www.themailboxb...

M000097207

The Mailbox® Monthly Idea Books— Your Ultimate Monthly Resource!

Your friends at *The Mailbox*® have taken monthly books to a whole new level! We've created a Web site that contains even more classroom resources to complement the hundreds of curriculum-based activities in each book. We've also added skill lines to each idea for a quick curriculum reference at a glance. Plus, every book has a comprehensive index to make planning and selecting activities even easier! All of these terrific features make this series of monthly books one that you can't be without!

Now Internet Interactive!

- For each book, you'll enjoy over **50 pages** of online resources, such as patterns, reproducibles, transparency masters, and classroom forms!
- You'll find **new** resources for **every** thematic unit in each book!
- Many classroom forms can be **filled out online** and printed. No more handwritten versions!
- Web site content is tailored to you and your **grade level.**
- **All** reproducibles and pattern pages from each monthly book are available online for **easy printing.**
- Access is absolutely **FREE!**

Getting your online extras is as easy as 1, 2, 3!

1. Go to **www.themailboxbooks.com** and click on "Add a book."
2. Complete the simple registration form.
3. Follow the on-screen instructions to add your book.

Look for the computer icon 💻 throughout each book to guide you to your FREE online extras.

About This Book

It's hard to believe we could improve on our best-selling series of monthly idea books—but we have! In this edition, you'll find the following exciting new features added to our irreplaceable collection of curriculum-based ideas!

- A Web site containing *even more* classroom resources complements the hundreds of activities provided in each book. (To access this incredible site for free, follow the simple instructions found on page 1.)
- A skill line for each idea provides a curriculum reference at a glance.
- A comprehensive index makes selecting and planning activities a breeze!

We think you'll agree that these new features make this series of monthly books the best ever!

Managing Editors: Cayce Guiliano, Scott Lyons

Editor at Large: Diane Badden

Contributing Writers: Becky Andrews, Beverly Cartledge, Chris Christensen, Ann Fisher, Beth Gress, Peggy W. Hambright, Paula Holdren, Elizabeth H. Lindsay, Thad McLaurin, Christa New, Christine A. Thuman

Copy Editors: Sylvan Allen, Lynn Bemer Coble, Gina Farago, Karen Brewer Grossman, Karen L. Huffman, Amy Kirtley-Hill, Carol Rawleigh, Jennifer Rudisill, Debbie Shoffner

Cover Artist: Clevell Harris

Art Coordinator: Theresa Lewis Goode

Artists: Jennifer T. Bennett, Pam Crane, Teresa Davidson, Theresa Lewis Goode, Nick Greenwood, Clevell Harris, Ivy L. Koonce, Sheila Krill, Clint Moore, Greg D. Rieves, Rebecca Saunders, Barry Slate, Donna K. Teal

Typesetters: Lynette Dickerson, David Jarrell, Mark Rainey

Indexer: Elizabeth Findley Caran

The Mailbox® Books.com: Kimberley Bruck (manager); Debra Liverman, Sharon Murphy (associate editors); Jennifer L. Tipton (designer/artist); Troy Lawrence, Stuart Smith (production artists); Karen White (editorial assistant); Paul Fleetwood, Xiaoyun Wu (systems)

President, The Mailbox Book Company™: Joseph C. Bucci

Director of Book Planning and Development: Chris Poindexter

Book Development Managers: Elizabeth H. Lindsay, Thad McLaurin, Susan Walker

Curriculum Director: Karen P. Shelton

Traffic Manager: Lisa K. Pitts

Librarian: Dorothy C. McKinney

Editorial and Freelance Management: Karen A. Brudnak

Editorial Training: Irving P. Crump

Editorial Assistants: Terrie Head, Hope Rodgers, Jan E. Witcher

Manufactured in the United States
10 9 8 7 6 5 4 3 2 1

FEBRUARY
Table of Contents

Online Extras 1

About This Book 2

February Planner Pages 4
Be prepared for a great month with these handy reproducibles.
- A teacher's resource list of February's special days
- A reproducible calendar of free-time activities for students
- A reproducible award and student desktag

Valentine's Day 8
Welcome this honey of a holiday into your classroom with curriculum-friendly activities.

African-American Heritage 22
Explore the inspiring history and heritage of African-Americans.

Chinese New Year 36
Celebrate with a festive array of educational activities. Happy New Year!

Friendship 42
Foster friendship and unity in your classroom with these friendly ideas.

Presidents of the United States 54
Use this executive lineup of activities to introduce your students to the more than 40 men who have been called "Mr. President."

Letter Writing 70
Deliver these first-class letter-writing activities to your class.

Weather 80
Don't wait for a rainy day to pull these magical weather activities from your hat!

Answer Keys 92

Index 94

Year of the Monkey Birthdays (1992)

Ben   Rashaun
Angie   Kim
Tonya   Keith

RAT   BOAR
OX   DOG
ROOSTER
MONKEY

FRIENDSHIP

U.S. Mail

February Calendar

Children's Dental Health Month

In observance of Children's Dental Health Month, invite a local dentist or dental hygienist to share the importance of good dental hygiene. After the visit, divide the class into small groups. Provide each group with poster board and markers. Instruct each group to create two posters—one depicting "Dental Dos" and another depicting "Dental Don'ts." Post these around the school to remind other students of good dental hygiene practices.

Canned Food Month

In honor of Canned Food Month, have your students contact a local soup kitchen or food pantry to inquire which canned goods are needed for the month of February. Then have students make posters requesting donations of those specific canned goods by a designated date. Select students to collect the cans from the other classrooms; then have parent volunteers deliver the cans to the appropriate organizations. Your students will feel proud of their contributions to the community.

1—Robinson Crusoe Day

Alexander Selkirk, a Scottish sailor, was rescued on this day in 1709 after being stranded on a deserted South Seas island for 52 months. Daniel Defoe based his classic book *Robinson Crusoe* on Selkirk's adventures. Have each student write about being stranded on an uninhabited island. Tell the student to explain where the island is located and how he will survive—what he will use for shelter, food, clothing, protection from beasts, etc. Encourage the student to illustrate his work.

2—Groundhog Day

Groundhog Day celebrates the belief that if the sun shines on Candlemas Day, or if the groundhog sees his shadow on this day, there will be six more weeks of winter. Punxsutawney, Pennsylvania, is famous for Punxsutawney Phil—a groundhog well known for his annual weather prediction. Have each student predict whether Phil will see his shadow or not. Then have each student keep track of the daily temperature and precipitation after February 2 to see if Phil's weather prediction was accurate.

3—Birthday of Elizabeth Blackwell

The first woman to become a medical doctor—Elizabeth Blackwell—was born on this day in 1821. Poll the students and record how many go to a male doctor and how many go to a female doctor. Then survey to determine how many students go to a male dentist and how many go to a female dentist. Graph the results. Have students draw conclusions from the graphed data.

7—Birthday of Laura Ingalls Wilder

Laura Ingalls Wilder was born on this day in 1867. Her famous Little House books describe her life growing up on the American prairie in the late 1800s. In celebration of her birthday, select one of Wilder's books as a read-aloud for February. Then have each student make a chart comparing the clothing, entertainment, chores, and games of a pioneer child of the late 1800s with that of a modern child.

National Pancake Week

This traditional celebration is observed the week of *Shrove* or *Pancake Tuesday* (the day before Ash Wednesday). Tell students that the largest pancake flipped on a griddle occurred on February 9, 1975. It was 12 feet in diameter! Recruit parent volunteers to treat your students to a pancake breakfast during National Pancake Week.

14—Ferris Wheel Day

George Washington Gale Ferris, born on this day in 1859, created the Ferris wheel for the World's Columbian Exposition held in Chicago in 1893. The wheel was 250 feet in diameter and contained 36 coaches—each capable of carrying 40 passengers. Have students share why they think Ferris wheels remain popular today despite the invention of faster rides.

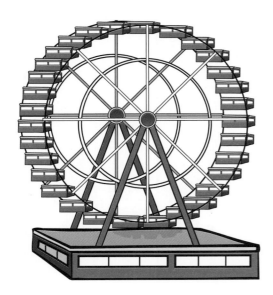

20—Student Volunteer Day

This day honors students who volunteer their free time to help improve the lives of others. Invite students to share how they have volunteered in their communities. Then have the class brainstorm specific ways it can volunteer in the school or community. Combine Student Volunteer Day with Canned Food Month for a very productive and rewarding February!

National Pencil Week

What would the world be like if the pencil hadn't been invented? In honor of National Pencil Week—the last full week of February—have students find out who invented the pencil, when it was invented, and when erasers were first added to the tops of pencils. For a fun activity, have each student write a story entitled "A Day in the Life of My Pencil," in which his pencil describes a typical day at school.

5

FREE-TIME FUN for February!

Tackle these 20 terrific tasks when you finish your work.

Monday	Tuesday	Wednesday	Thursday	Friday
February is Snack Food Month. List your favorite snacks. What makes you a healthful *snacker?*	Create a new invention for National New Idea Week. Draw a diagram of your invention and describe its purpose.	P. T. Barnum bought the famous elephant Jumbo in 1882. Write about your favorite circus animal and include an illustration.	No American woman is honored by a national holiday. Pick an American female and tell why she should be honored.	In 1919, an act of Congress established the Grand Canyon as a national park. List the national parks you've visited and their locations.
For National Crime Prevention Week, write a paragraph about how you can keep from being a victim of crime.	In 1877, the empress of Brazil gave Queen Victoria a dress made of spiderwebs. Design an outfit using things found in nature.	For Girls and Women in Sports Day, brainstorm a list of women's sports. List the top five female athletes of each sport.	Many presidents enjoyed participating in sports. List five presidents and their favorite sports.	Laredo, Texas, has a Jalapeño Festival in February. *Jalapeños* are hot peppers. Describe the spiciest meal you've ever eaten.
George Washington's meals often had eight meat dishes! Describe the biggest meal you've ever eaten.	In honor of Potato Lovers Month, describe the most unusual way you have eaten a potato.	*The American Magazine*, America's first magazine, was published on February 13, 1741. Describe your favorite magazine.	Valentine's Day is February 14. Create a card for a friend or family member. Write an original poem inside.	In 1939, Walt Disney's *Snow White and the Seven Dwarfs* won an award for excellence. List your favorite animated movies.
King Tut's tomb was opened in 1923. It had remained undisturbed since the 14th century B.C. Estimate how many years it was undisturbed.	The first "Great Five-Cent Store" opened in 1879. A nickel could buy a baseball in 1879. Make a list of things five cents will buy today.	On Hoodie Hoo Day people of the Northern Hemisphere go outside and yell "Hoodie Hoo" to chase winter away. List other holidays that welcome spring.	In 1971, Kirt Barnes iceskated 100 miles in less than six hours. Calculate Barnes's average speed while skating.	Leap Year gives February a 29th day every four years. How would you feel if your birthday were on the 29th and only came every four years?

6

©The Education Center, Inc. • FEBRUARY • TEC207

Note to the teacher: Have each student staple a copy of this page inside a file folder. Direct students to store their completed work inside their folders.

Desktag: Duplicate student copies on construction paper. Have each student personalize and decorate his pattern; then laminate the patterns and use them as desktags during February.

Award: Duplicate multiple copies. Keep them handy at your desk during the month of February. When a student earns an award, write her name on the appropriate line. Special prizes can be given with the awards.

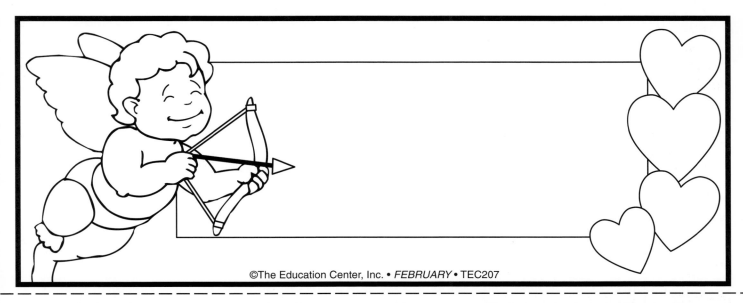

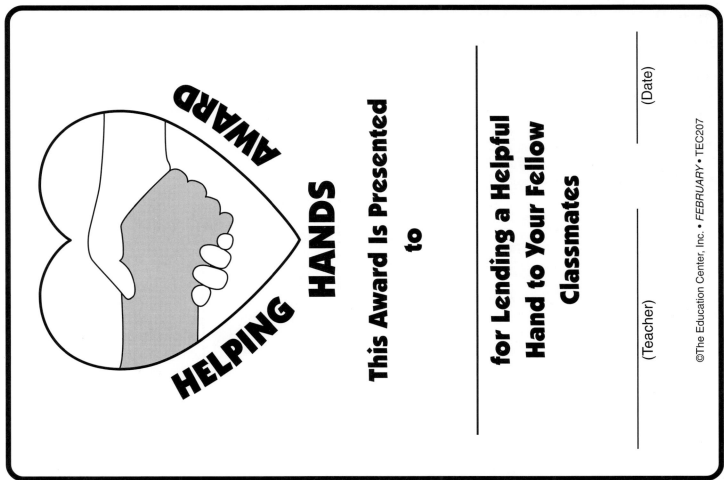

HELPING HANDS AWARD

This Award Is Presented

to

for Lending a Helpful
Hand to Your Fellow
Classmates

(Teacher)

(Date)

A HONEY OF A HOLIDAY

Easy and Educational Activities for Valentine's Day

Hearts, hugs, happy smiles, heavenly tasting candy—put them all together and you've got everyone's favorite February holiday! Welcome Valentine's Day with open arms and the following curriculum-friendly activities and reproducibles!

by Chris Christensen and Ann Fisher

A Dilution Solution
Observing changes in molecules

Add a sip of science to your Valentine's Day activities with this hands-on demonstration. First show students a half-filled cup of clear soda pop (such as 7-Up® or Sprite®). Add two drops of red food coloring to the cup. After students have noted the change in the color of the liquid, pour it into a large clear bowl. Next add one can of the clear soda pop to the bowl at a time until the red color disappears. Ask students, "Where did the red coloring go?" Have each student answer this question in his science journal. Then explain that the red was visible in the cup of tinted soda because there was a close ratio between the food coloring molecules and the soda molecules. As you began to add additional soda to the mixture, the presence of more soda molecules increased the ratio. The red molecules had to spread out. Finally, because the red molecules were so small and spread so far apart, they became invisible. After discussing this demonstration with the class, distribute paper cups and let students enjoy a sip of their science!

Valentine Symmetry
Practicing symmetry

Sneak a little math into your Valentine's Day party without anyone noticing! Have parent volunteers bring in undecorated heart-shaped cookies (one per student) and tubes of pink, red, and white squeezable frosting or decorating gel. Review the concept of *symmetry* with your class; then challenge each student to use the frosting to decorate her cookie with a symmetrical design. After having a partner check her cookie's design, direct each child to snack on her symmetrical sweet!

Love Patches Things Up!
Narrative writing

Writing and art go hand in hand in this eye-catching Valentine's Day display! Cut a giant red heart from bulletin board paper. Draw several lines on the heart to make it appear as if it's been broken; then cut on the lines. Reassemble the heart on a bulletin board or wall as shown. Add the title "Love Patches Things Up!"

Next, lead a class discussion about the different forms love can take: a kind deed, the sacrifice of your wishes for those of a loved one, a word of encouragement when a friend is sad, etc. Talk about how love can mend broken friendships and patch up misunderstandings. Then have each student cut a 4" x 4" square of notebook paper. On the square, have the student write about a time when he experienced, initiated, or witnessed a loving act. Next have the student cut a 5" x 5" piece of construction paper and trim its edges with pinking shears. Have the student decorate the resulting patch; then have him tape it to the top of his written square. Staple each finished patch (at the top only) to the bulletin board as shown. Each morning during February, read aloud one or two of the paragraphs from the display. Discuss how love patched up the particular problem or helped those involved.

Holiday Writing Center 🖥
Writing for a variety of purposes

Looking for a writing center that your students are sure to be sweet on this February? The pattern on page 15, the list of terrific writing assignments below, and the following directions make this center a sweet—and simple—success!

Preparing the center: Make ten copies of the task card pattern on page 15 on pink, red, or lavender paper. Label each card with one of the tasks below. At your center, hang red and pink crepe-paper streamers from the ceiling or wall. Display the task cards (laminated if desired) in a basket decorated with a red bow, an empty Valentine's Day candy box, or an inverted red umbrella.

Making writing booklets: Have each student cut out two identical large hearts from red construction paper. Then have him trace one of the hearts on several sheets of notebook paper, cut out the tracings, and staple them between his two heart covers. Encourage each student to personalize the cover of his booklet and complete the center's writing assignments inside it.

Tasks:

• Create a sentence with each word beginning with a letter in the word *valentine*. For example: <u>V</u>an and <u>L</u>il <u>e</u>at <u>n</u>ine <u>t</u>omatoes <u>i</u>nside <u>N</u>ana's <u>e</u>levator.

• Research the human heart. Inside your booklet, list ten new facts you learned from your research.

• Invent a new Valentine's Day candy! Write a description of your creation's ingredients. Then write a commercial message describing your scrumptious treat.

• In your booklet, write a thank-you note to someone at school who has helped you in some way. Then make a Valentine's Day card in which you can copy the note. Deliver the card to your friend.

• Someone has sent you a very special Valentine's Day gift. There was no name on the card. Write your strategy for finding out the identity of your secret admirer.

• Pretend that you are a delicious, cherry-flavored Valentine's Day lollipop. Write a journal entry describing your life from the factory to a tummy.

• Valentine's Day is a holiday that focuses on feelings from the heart. What do you wish for most—from the bottom of your heart? Describe your wish in a paragraph.

• How is the emotion of *love* like the emotion of *hate?* How are they different? Write a paragraph that compares and contrasts these two emotions.

• In a paragraph, describe a food that you just *love.* But in your description, do not name the food. Give the description to a classmate. Can he or she guess the identity of the food?

• What famous person would you just *love* to get a valentine from? Write a paragraph that explains why you would like to hear from this person on Valentine's Day.

Invent a new Valentine's Day candy! Write a description of your creation's ingredients. Then write a commercial message describing your scrumptious treat.

Valentine's Day is a holiday that focuses on feelings from the heart. What do you wish for most—from the bottom of your heart? Describe your wish in a paragraph.

Prominent Pairs 🖥

Using deductive reasoning

Romeo and Juliet, Kermit® and Miss Piggy®, Beauty and the Beast—Valentine's Day often reminds us of those famous pairs who grace the pages of favorite books or the big screen. Sharpen critical- and creative-thinking skills with this fun game based on notable twosomes. Have students brainstorm a list of famous pairs; then record these pairs on the chalkboard (see the suggestions below). Ask a student volunteer to write the name of each member from a pair on a separate slip of paper. Shuffle the slips; then pin one slip to the back of each child's shirt so that only his classmates can see the name on the slip. Direct your students to circulate around the room. Instruct each child to try to identify the name on his back and to try to find his partner by asking only yes-and-no questions of his classmates. When a pair has been identified, allow those partners to circle their names on the chalkboard's list. Then have the partners return to the game to help their classmates complete the challenge.

Romeo & Juliet	Bill & Hillary Clinton	Beauty & the Beast
Kermit® & Miss Piggy®	Bert® & Ernie®	Mickey® & Minnie® Mouse
Pat Sajak & Vanna White	Road Runner™ & Coyote™	King Ferdinand & Queen Isabella
Batman® & Robin™	Charlie Brown™ & Lucy™	Tweetie Bird & Sylvester®
Garfield® & Odie®	Jack & Jill	Ben & Jerry
Lois Lane® & Clark Kent™	Hansel & Gretel	Pocahontas & John Smith

Spin to Win!

Recognizing positive behaviors

Need a fun game for your Valentine's Day party or a February Friday afternoon? Look no more! Have each child cut out 12 one-inch hearts from red or pink construction paper. Then divide the class into groups of four students each. Give each group one copy of the gameboard on page 16.

To begin play, each student places six of her hearts in the middle of the table to make a game pile. In turn, each player uses a paper clip and pencil point as shown on the gameboard to spin. After spinning, she follows the directions written on the space where the paper clip has landed. Players draw only from the game pile for any "collect" commands. Hearts lost due to "lose" commands go in the game pile as well. If a player loses all of her hearts, she is out of the game. The last student to remain in the game wins.

Riddle Me This! 💻

Conducting an experiment, observing a chemical reaction

Fill February with some hands-on science your students will love! Purchase seven large, red (preferably heart-shaped) balloons. Blow up each balloon; then twist the opening and secure it closed with a twist tie. Use a red pen or fine-tipped marker to label each balloon in tiny letters with the answer to one of the Valentine's Day riddles below. Remove the twist tie so the balloon will deflate. Next write the balloon's riddle on a small index card. Carefully paper-clip the card to the deflated balloon.

On the day of this activity, divide the class into seven groups. Give each group a balloon, its matching riddle card, and the following materials and list of steps:

Materials: clear, 1-liter, plastic bottle; 1 teaspoon baking soda; 3 tablespoons vinegar in a small paper cup; masking tape; sheet of notebook paper

Read the riddle card aloud. Try to solve the riddle. Then follow the steps below to check the answer.

Steps:

1. Roll and tape the paper to make a cone shape, with a small opening at the tip.
2. Pour the baking soda into the bottle using the paper cone.
3. Carefully pour the vinegar into the opening of the balloon.
4. Stretch the open end of the balloon over the mouth of the bottle. Make sure that the balloon droops over the side of the bottle so that the vinegar doesn't go into the bottle.
5. Tape the open end of the balloon to the bottle to secure the balloon in place.
6. Slowly lift the balloon so that the vinegar pours into the bottle. Observe what happens.

Results: The vinegar–baking soda mixture will begin to bubble, indicating that a chemical change is taking place. The baking soda–and–vinegar mix will create carbon dioxide gas, thus causing the balloon to inflate with the CO_2. When this happens, the group will be able to read the answer to its riddle on the balloon!

Valentine's Day Riddles

- What did the love letter say to the stamp? *You send me!*
- What did the stamp say to the envelope? *I'm stuck on you!*
- What is an iceman's favorite love song? *"I Only Have Ice for You, Dear"*
- What did the boy octopus say to the girl octopus? *May I hold your hand, hand, hand, hand, hand, hand, hand, hand?*
- What do squirrels give each other for Valentine's Day? *"Forget-me-nuts"*
- What does a vampire call his sweetheart? *His "ghoul-friend"*
- What did the lovesick potato say to his sweetheart? *I only have eyes for you!*

Candy Heart Graphing
Collecting and graphing data

Make math a treat with this oh-so-sweet graphing activity. Purchase a supply of candy hearts so that each child has enough to fill a small plastic bag. Also tape together eight to ten sheets of one-inch graph paper as shown. Along the left side of the far left sheet of paper, color in one square for each color of hearts; then draw a dividing line to separate these squares from the rest of the display as shown. Post the display (soon to be a giant bar graph) on a bulletin board or wall.

Distribute the bags of candy to the class. Direct each child to predict the most frequent color found in his bag of hearts without closely examining its contents. Record these predictions on the chalkboard. Next have each child count each color of hearts in his bag, keeping a tally on a sheet of paper. Instruct the student to bring his completed tally sheet to the graph and color in one square for each heart of each color in his bag. After each student has had an opportunity to add his tallies to the graph, check to see whether the students' earlier predictions were accurate. As a follow-up, have students challenge each other with original word problems based on the graph's information.

Seeing Red!
Understanding vocabulary

Haven't got the heart to make students endure boring vocabulary drills? Then introduce them instead to the very vivid vocabulary of Valentine's Day! Begin by having students brainstorm a list of words or phrases that include the word *heart* (*heartburn, heart-to-heart, hearty,* etc.). List their responses on a sheet of chart paper. Have dictionaries handy so students can read aloud the definitions of unknown words or expressions. Post the list so that students can use the words in their Valentine's Day writing activities (see "Holiday Writing Center" on page 10).

Follow up this brainstorming session by having students investigate expressions containing the word *red* with the reproducible activity on page 19. Or let them tackle the reproducible wordplay activity found on page 20.

Have a Heart! 🖥

Solving multiplication problems

Sharpen multiplication and thinking skills with this exciting game! Have each pair of students cut out nine small hearts from red paper; then have the pair label each heart with a numeral from 1–6, 8–9, and 0. Provide a zippered plastic bag in which the pair can store its hearts, a pair of dice, a small copy of a multiplication table, and a copy of these game instructions:

How to play:

1. Place the hearts, numeral-side-up, on the desk.
2. Player One rolls the dice, multiplies the two numbers showing, and announces the answer.
3. Player Two checks Player One's answer with the multiplication table. If incorrect, Player Two takes a turn. If correct, Player One removes the cut-out hearts that match the answer's digits. (For example, if a 4 and a 6 are rolled, the player announces that the product is 24. He then removes the 2 heart and the 4 heart from the desk.)
4. Player One continues until he either gives an incorrect answer or cannot remove any hearts from the desk. To determine his score for this round, Player One adds the numerals on the hearts that remain on the desk.
5. Return all of the hearts, numeral-side-up, to the desk. Player Two then takes a turn, following steps 2–4.
6. At the end of ten rounds, the player with the *lowest* score wins.

A Heartfelt Greeting

Experiencing a cultural tradition

Here's an easy project that makes a great Valentine's Day gift for your students. (Or have each student make one to give to her parents.) Duplicate one copy of the heart pattern on page 15 on white construction paper for each child. Then follow these simple instructions to make one greeting:

Materials: 16" length of gathered white lace, 1" wide; 5" length of red or pink ribbon, 1/4" wide; glue; Valentine's Day lollipop or pencil; scissors; pencil; markers or crayons

Steps:

1. Cut out the heart shape. Use markers or crayons to add color to it.
2. Glue the lace around the edge of the heart.
3. After the lace has dried, tie a small bow with the red or pink ribbon; then glue it to the bottom point of the heart as shown.
4. Sign your name to the greeting.
5. Gently poke a pencil through the two hole markers on the heart. Insert the Valentine's Day lollipop or pencil through the holes.

This little card
Is meant to say
That you are thought of
In a special way!

Happy Valentine's Day!

Love,
Eva

©The Education Center, Inc. • *FEBRUARY* • TEC207

Pattern
Use with "A Heartfelt Greeting" on page 14.

This little card
Is meant to say
That you are thought of
In a special way!

Happy Valentine's Day!

Love,

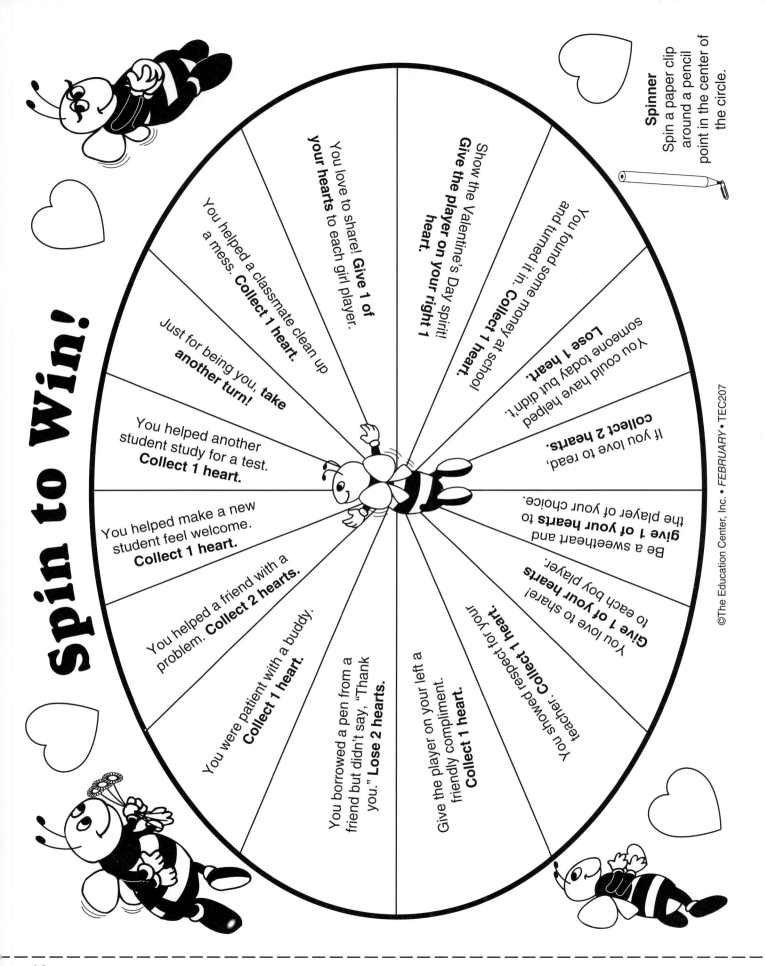

Spin to Win!

Spinner
Spin a paper clip around a pencil point in the center of the circle.

You love to share! **Give 1 of your hearts** to each girl player.

Show the Valentine's Day spirit! **Give the player on your right 1 heart.**

You helped a classmate clean up a mess. **Collect 1 heart.**

You found some money and turned it in. **Collect 1 heart.**

Just for being you, **take another turn!**

You could have helped someone today but didn't. **Lose 1 heart.**

You helped another student study for a test. **Collect 1 heart.**

If you love to read, **collect 2 hearts.**

You helped make a new student feel welcome. **Collect 1 heart.**

Be a sweetheart and **give 1 of your hearts to** the player of your choice.

You helped a friend with a problem. **Collect 2 hearts.**

You love to share! **Give 1 of your hearts** to each boy player.

You were patient with a buddy. **Collect 1 heart.**

You showed respect for your teacher. **Collect 1 heart.**

You borrowed a pen from a friend but didn't say, "Thank you." **Lose 2 hearts.**

Give the player on your left a friendly compliment. **Collect 1 heart.**

©The Education Center, Inc. • *FEBRUARY* • TEC207

Note to the teacher: Use this gameboard with "Spin to Win!" on page 11. Make one copy for each group of four students.

Pointing Toward Patterns

It's February, and that means that Cupid is just swamped, busily slinging his arrows here and there! Along his way, Cupid managed to shoot this patterning activity in your direction.

Directions: Study each row and decide on the pattern. Then continue each pattern by filling in the blank or blanks after it.

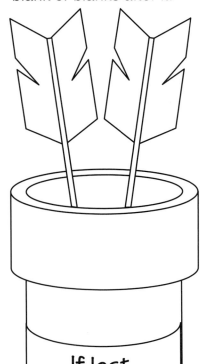

1. XO   XOO   XOOO   ____   ____   ____

2.    ____

3.    ____   ____   ____

4. CU   UP   PI   ____

5. (7, 14)   (14, 14)   (21, 14)   (28, 14)   ____   ____

6.    ____   ____

7.   ____

8.   ____   ____

9.   ____   ____

10.   ____

11. 2,   8,   20,   44,   ____   ____

12. (ZA)   (BY)   (XC)   ____   ____   ____

Bonus Box: On the back of this page, create three of your own Valentine's Day patterns for a friend to finish.

Simply Sweethearts

Mel and Millie had a terrific idea. They decided to open up a new store called "Simply Sweethearts." It sells items for people to give to their sweeties on Valentine's Day and other special occasions. Before Mel and Millie opened their store, they surveyed a group of people to find out the kinds of valentine gifts they gave last year. Mel and Millie made a pie graph to show the data they collected. Look at it carefully as you answer the questions below.
Hint: It may help to first convert all the fractions to ones with a common denominator.

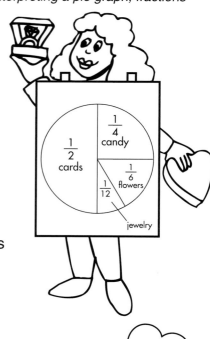

A. Mel and Millie surveyed 120 people.
　1. What number of people gave Valentine's Day cards? _____
　2. What number gave flowers? _____
　3. How many more people gave candy than jewelry? _____

B. Suppose that Mel and Millie surveyed only 60 people.
　4. How many people gave candy? _____
　5. How many people gave their sweethearts jewelry? _____
　6. What total number of people gave cards, flowers, and jewelry? _____

C. Suppose that Mel and Millie really got cracking and surveyed 360 people.
　7. How many people gave flowers? _____
　8. How many more people gave cards than candy? _____
　9. How many fewer people gave jewelry than flowers? _____

D. Now pretend that Mel and Millie were able to survey only 48 people.
　10. How many people did not give candy? _____
　11. How many people did not give jewelry? _____
　12. How many did not give cards or flowers? _____

E. Finally, determine how many people were surveyed if:
　13. 30 people gave candy: _____
　14. 100 gave flowers: _____
　15. 40 gave flowers: _____
　16. 120 gave cards: _____
　17. 100 gave jewelry: _____
　18. 150 gave candy: _____

Bonus Box: Out of 90 people surveyed about the gifts they received last Valentine's Day, 10 received perfume, 10 received concert tickets, 10 received CDs, 15 received flowers, 15 received cards, and 30 received candy. On the back of this paper, draw a pie graph with fractions like the one shown above for these statistics.

Seeing Red!

Valentine's Day is the one day of the year on which you're guaranteed to see red! Many expressions found in our language include the word *red*. Some of their meanings may surprise you! Read each sentence below. Use a dictionary to help you find the meaning of each boldfaced word or phrase. After you have located the meaning, color the heart and write your answer in the blank.

1. Would an office worker likely think that lots of **red tape** was pretty? _____

2. If you received a **redingote** as a gift, would you eat it, wear it, or read it? _____

3. Is a **redbreast** a type of flower, food, or bird? _____

4. Was last Valentine's Day a **red-letter** day for you? _____ Explain your answer. _____
_____
_____

5. Does news that is **red-hot** mean that it is up-to-the-minute news that everyone would want to know? Or is it news that will probably interest only a few people? _____

6. Describe a time when you were caught **red-handed:**
_____

7. In what war did the **redcoats** fight? _____

8. Would a **red cap** work at a grocery store, mall, or railroad station? _____

9. Where is the **Red Sea** located? _____

10. Would you give the president the **red-carpet** treatment if he visited your school? _____

11. If the captain of your army unit put you on **red alert,** would you be nervous or joyful? _____

12. Does a **red giant** have something to do with the land, sky, or oceans? _____

13. What flavor is usually associated with a **red-hot** candy? _____

14. If your business were in the **red,** would you be happy or worried? _____

15. If someone is boring or dull, would he or she be described as **red-blooded?** _____

> **Bonus Box:** What color would you use to describe yourself? Write a paragraph on the back of this page explaining why you chose your color and how it best describes you.

Note to the teacher: Use with "Seeing Red!" on page 13.

Valentine Word Chains

Poor Cupid! He started a job he can't seem to finish. For each word below, Cupid wants to change one letter at a time to form a new word. His goal is to form four different chains of 14 linking words each. But he needs your help. Follow these guidelines to help Cupid complete his chains:

1. Don't change the same letter twice in a row. For example, don't change LOVE to LONE and then to LOBE. Instead, change LOVE to LONE and then to LANE.
2. Don't repeat any word within a chain.
3. Keep a dictionary handy to check words.
4. If you need more space, continue the chain on the back of this page.

LOVE   GIFT   ROSE   HEART

Bonus Box: Suppose that you are starting a new chain with the word SWEET. How many different words can you list for the second word in the chain? Write them on the back of this page.

Patchwork Patterns

After a full day of shooting arrows at lovesick sweethearts, Cupid is pooped! He's ready to hit the sack under his favorite quilt—the one with all the broken hearts. Mend each heart on the quilt by drawing a line to connect its halves so that each "mended" heart in a patch follows a certain rule. For example, if the rule that connects the hearts in one patch is "add 1," you would draw a line to connect 3 with 4, 7 with 8, and so on. After you've connected the heart halves in a patch, write its rule in the blank. The rule is different in each patch. Be careful—there is an extra heart half in each patch!

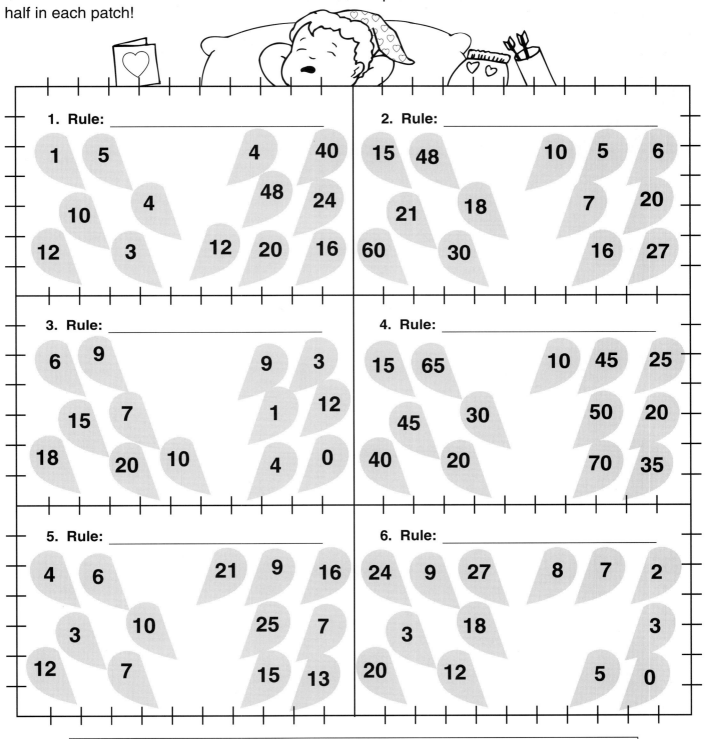

Bonus Box: Add the next three numbers in this number pattern: 2, 6, 4, 12, 10, ___, ___, ___.

A Heroic Heritage
Activities to Celebrate the History and the Accomplishments of African Americans

Unlike other immigrants who journeyed to the United States, most African Americans arrived as captives and were sold into slavery. Use the following activities to help your students understand the inspiring and courageous history of African Americans.

by Beth Gress and Thad H. McLaurin

Triangular Trade
Understanding the importance of historical events

What do ships, rum, Africa, molasses, the West Indies, slaves, and America have in common? Each was a major factor in the *triangle trade route.* The triangle trade route was a three-stage trading system responsible for bringing 8 to 15 million captive Africans to the New World between the 16th and the 19th centuries. First British ships loaded with rum, iron goods, and guns sailed from America to the West African coast, where they traded their cargo for captured Africans. Next the captive Africans endured a grueling journey known as the "middle passage" to the West Indies, where they were traded for molasses. Finally, the slave ships traveled to New England, where the remaining Africans were sold into slavery and the molasses was made into rum. Use one or more of the activities below to help students gain a better understanding of the triangle trade route.

- Have students research why rum, iron goods, and guns were so important to the African slave traders.
- Read the following passage written by Olaudah Equiano—an 11-year-old African boy who survived the grueling "middle passage":
  "The closeness of the place and the number of us crowded so closely together almost suffocated us. The horrible smells made the air unfit to breathe. This brought on sickness that killed many of us."
- Ask students to name the feelings and emotions conveyed in the passage. Then have each student write a journal entry answering such questions as "What would you do if you were suddenly kidnapped and taken from your family?" and "How would you feel if you did not know whether you would ever see your family again?" Have volunteers share their entries.
- Read aloud one of the books listed below. Each tells a unique story of the trials Africans endured when captured and transported to America. As students listen to the story, have them record reflections in their journals.
  — *The Slave Dancer* by Paula Fox
  — *Ajeemah and His Son* by James Berry
  — *The Story of the Amistad* by Emma Gelders Sterne

Black History Contracts

Acknowledging contributions in history, researching a topic

What is *ethnic pride?* Who were the important leaders of the civil rights movement? Help your students find the answers to these and other questions related to Black American history by completing the following independent activities. Duplicate a class set of pages 31–33. Direct each student to select a Black American achiever from page 33 to use with the activities on page 32. Provide a variety of resources and literature books for students to use. After each student has completed pages 31 and 32, check the answers for page 31 and have each student share two of his "Black American Achievers Contract" activities with the class. Display the completed contract projects around the classroom.

Here are some suggested books to include:

* *One More River to Cross: The Story of Twelve Black Americans* by Jim Haskins
* *Afro-Bets® Book of Black Heroes From A to Z: An Introduction to Important Black Achievers* by Wade Hudson and Valerie W. Wesley
* *Book of Black Heroes Vol. 2: Great Women in the Struggle* by Toyomi Igus
* *Now Is Your Time! The African American Struggle for Freedom* by Walter Dean Myers

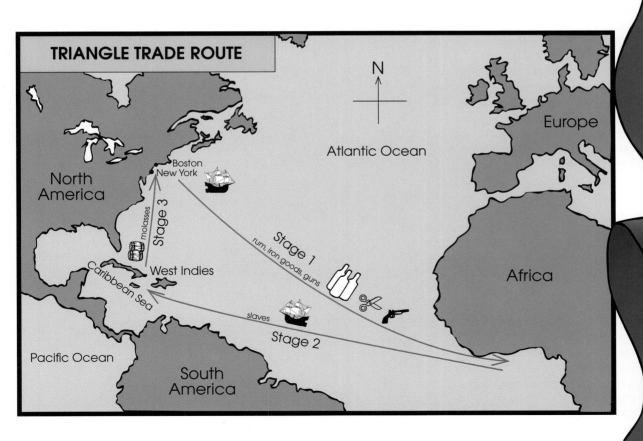

Adire T-Shirts 🖥

Experiencing a cultural tradition, following directions

The art of making *adire* or tie-dyed T-shirts is very popular in West Africa. Have each student follow the directions below to create his own adire T-shirt. Encourage students to wear their finished shirts to schoolwide black history events.

Materials:
- prewashed, 100% cotton T-shirt for each student
- nylon sewing thread and sewing needles
- rubber bands
- yardstick
- scissors
- pencils
- 2 buttons per student
- blue fabric dye (follow the directions on the package)
- 2 or 3 large buckets, each containing the prepared dye
- warm water for the dye; cool water for the rinse
- plastic drop cloth or shower curtain

Student directions:
1. Use a pencil to draw a straight, wavy, or zigzag line across the front of your T-shirt as shown.
2. Measure and cut a three-foot length of thread. Thread your needle and tie a button to the end of the thread as shown.
3. Sew along the pencil line using a running stitch—over, under, over, under. Make sure to pierce the needle through both the front and back layers of fabric as shown.
4. After you finish sewing the line, tie a second button to the end of the thread.
5. Gather the fabric along the thread; then tie the ends of the thread together tightly as shown.
6. Make several tufts of the remaining fabric and wrap them tightly with rubber bands as shown.
7. Place the dye buckets on the plastic cloth.
8. Slowly push your T-shirt down into a bucket of dye.
9. Soak the shirt for three to five minutes.
10. Rinse the T-shirt in cool water and hang it to drip-dry over the plastic.
11. When the T-shirt is dry, cut and remove the thread; then remove the rubber bands.

Helpful hint to the teacher: Heat set the dye and remove the wrinkles by placing the dried shirts in a clothes dryer along with a wet towel.

The Ladder of Leadership

Acknowledging contributions in history, researching a topic

What is a *leader?* Have students brainstorm definitions of leader. Summarize that a leader is "someone who has authority and influence in the community, county, state, country, or world." Stock a center with various newsmagazines and newspapers. Then instruct each student to look through these and other resources for articles about current black leaders. Instruct each student to read about one leader and then write a short paragraph explaining why that person is a good leader. Have each student present his paragraph. Then have the class organize the leaders into categories based on professions, such as politics, entertainment, education, sports, and science (see page 33 for possible categories). Create a banner for each category. Then display each paragraph under the correct banner on a bulletin board titled "Leading the Way."

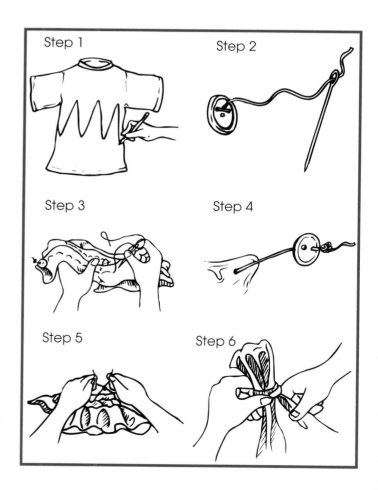

Step 1 Step 2 Step 3 Step 4 Step 5 Step 6

African American Authors

Introduce your students to this collection of stories by African American authors. The art, literature, and culture of the people will come alive with these books and activities.

Follow the Drinking Gourd
by Jeanette Winter
Understanding the times in which people lived through song

The concept of slavery and the desire for freedom are explained in this easy-to-understand story. Students will appreciate the importance of the Underground Railroad and the bravery of those who dared to travel it.

The music to "Follow the Drinking Gourd" is written in the back of the book. Enlist the help of your music teacher to teach your children the words and melody of the song. Then divide the song into sections and have students create illustrations to go with the lyrics. Have your students perform the song for another class in celebration of Black History Month. Let the illustrators share their pictures at the appropriate times in the performance.

Honey, I Love
by Eloise Greenfield
Making a personal connection

A sweet and simple story told in rhyme, *Honey, I Love* is a tribute to the little pleasures in life. Share the story with your students; then have them add to the list by naming things that bring them joy. Have each student make a poster of pictures and phrases of things that give him happiness. Post these in your room to remind everyone of life's simple pleasures.

Cornrows
by Camille Yarbrough
Experiencing a cultural tradition

The significance of braiding hair into cornrows is explained in this story-within-a-story. To prepare, display a map of Africa; then have students locate the countries mentioned as you read the story.

After the story, teach your children the art of braiding by making friendship bracelets. Give each student three 12-inch pieces of yarn. Show students how to overlap the pieces into a braided string. Each student can trade his braided-yarn bracelet with another student, and they can tie the braids around their wrists to signify friendship.

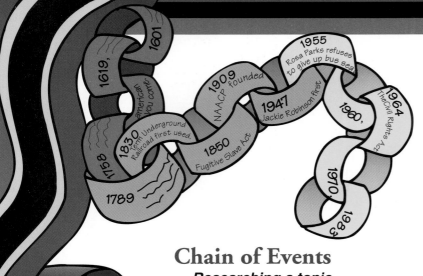

Chain of Events
Researching a topic, sequencing events

Each historical event creates a new link in the chain of history. Help students visualize the African American saga by creating a chain of events. Duplicate page 30; then cut it into the designated eight sections. Divide students into eight groups and give each group one section from page 30. Distribute four 2" x 12" strips of colored paper and markers to each group. Instruct each group to research the dates and other interesting facts of the four events listed on its section. Using a different strip for each historical event, have group members write the date of the event, copy the sentence from the section you gave them, and add one more fact to each strip. When the strips are completed, have the class help you arrange them in chronological order (see page 92 for dates). Enlist two or three students to assemble the strips into a chain. Glue the ends of the first strip together, creating a ring with the writing visible on the outside. Insert one end of the next strip through the center of the first ring. Then glue the ends of the second strip together, creating two links of a chain. Continue adding links until each strip has been attached. Share this newfound knowledge by hanging the black history chain around the classroom, over the door, or above a bulletin board.

"Follow the Drinking Gourd"
Understanding the times in which people lived through song

Southern slaves risked extreme danger and even death escaping to freedom. Many slaves followed the Underground Railroad—a secret network of people and hiding places. A sailor named Peg Leg Joe helped many slaves travel the Underground Railroad. He worked on plantations as a handyman, befriending the slaves and teaching them the words to the folk song "Follow the Drinking Gourd." The song seemed harmless to the plantation owners, but hidden in its lyrics were directions for escaping to freedom.

Read aloud the picture book *Follow the Drinking Gourd* by Jeanette Winter. Then read the verses of the folk song printed in the back of the book. Divide students into eight groups. Assign two groups to each of the three verses and two groups to the chorus. Give each group a big piece of poster board and markers. Instruct each group to illustrate the hidden messages of its assigned verse or chorus. If needed, have groups use the book as a reference for their illustrations. Enlist your music teacher to teach students the song's melody. Once each group has completed its poster, have the students perform the folk song for another class. During the song, direct a representative from each group to hold up its poster at the appropriate verse or chorus. At the end of the song, have each group share additional details about the hidden messages illustrated on its poster.

Jackie Robinson
Acknowledging contributions in history, researching a topic

Jackie Robinson knew he needed more than athletic skill to be the first African American to play major-league baseball. He also needed the dignity to stand by his beliefs and the strength to remain composed under pressure. Read aloud chapter 6 of the novel *In the Year of the Boar and Jackie Robinson* by Betty B. Lord. Share the following quote from the same chapter:

"This year, Jackie Robinson is at bat. He stands for himself, for Americans of every hue, for an America that honors fair play."

Have students explain what the quote means. Discuss why Jackie Robinson is considered by many to be a hero. Then ask students, "What makes Jackie Robinson a hero?", "Is every professional athlete a hero?", and "Which other black athletes have been considered heroes and why?" Next divide the class into 12 groups. Assign each group one of the athletes listed below to research. Give each group one 12" x 18" sheet of light-colored paper and markers. Then have each group design the paper to look like a picture frame. Have each group illustrate its athlete in the center of the frame and then list the major accomplishments and contributions of the athlete around the border of the frame. After each group presents its framed portrait, display the pictures around the classroom.

Henry Aaron	Joe Louis
Arthur Ashe	Willie Mays
Wilt Chamberlain	Jesse Owens
Althea Gibson	Satchel Paige
Jackie Joyner-Kersee	Sugar Ray Robinson
Sugar Ray Leonard	Wilma Rudolph

African American Achievers' Hall of Fame
Acknowledging contributions in history, researching a topic

From theater to business, many professions have been impacted by the contributions of African Americans. Help students comprehend the contributions of African Americans by creating an "African American Achievers' Hall of Fame." Divide students into 12 groups. Duplicate one copy of page 33 for each group and one copy of page 34 for each student. Assign one category from page 33 to each group. Instruct each group to select at least two people from its assigned category. Tell each group to complete one copy of page 34 for each selected African American achiever.

To display each group's work, write the name of each category from page 33 on a separate 6" x 24" piece of brightly colored paper; then post the category names in the hallway. Have each group present its inductees' information sheets. Then mount each sheet on colored paper and post it underneath the appropriate category.

The First African American

Major League Baseball Player

Jackie Robinson

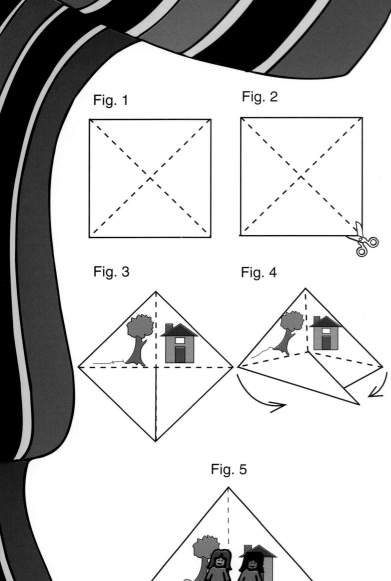

Fig. 1

Fig. 2

Fig. 3

Fig. 4

Fig. 5

Fig. 6

Cousins by Virginia Hamilton

Black Author "Quadramas" 🖥

Reading independently, identifying story plot

Expose your students to the wide variety of African American books by creating an African American authors center. Stock the center with books that students can read in the center or check out for several days. Below is a list of children's authors who would be appropriate for the center. After a student reads a book, instruct him to construct a *"quadrama"* (see the instructions below). Display the "quadramas" around the classroom to inspire students to read more books by African American authors.

James Berry	Virginia Hamilton
Candy Dawson Boyd	Jim Haskins
Deborah M. Newton	Langston Hughes
Chocolate	Fredrick McKissack
Lucille Clifton	Patricia C. McKissack
Ossie Davis	Walter Dean Myers
Tom Feelings	John Steptoe
Nikki Giovanni	Mildred D. Taylor
Eloise Greenfield	

Materials for each student: four 9" x 9" pieces of white paper, two 8 1/2" x 11" sheets of white construction paper, scissors, glue, markers, tape

Directions:

1. Fold a 9" x 9" piece of paper diagonally as shown (Figure 1).
2. Open and cut along one fold line, stopping at the center (Figure 2).
3. Repeat Steps 1 and 2 with the other three sheets.
4. Illustrate one scene from the novel on each 9" x 9" square (Figure 3).
5. Overlap the two bottom triangles of each square and secure them with glue or tape (Figure 4).
6. Add stand-up characters or scenery to make each scene three-dimensional (Figure 5).
7. Write a brief description of each scene (Figure 6).
8. Include the title and author of the book on one of the scenes.
9. Glue the backs of each scene together, creating a pyramid as shown.

Dahomey Appliqués
Making a personal connection

The Dahomey people of West Africa passed on their cultural heritage through colorful appliqués. Have each student tell about his family by creating his own Dahomey appliqué (see the directions below). Then inspire each student to explain the symbols on his completed wall hanging.

Materials for each student: 12" x 18" piece of black paper, five or six 9" x 12" assorted colored pieces of paper, assorted colored markers or crayons, scissors, glue, black marker or crayon

Directions:
1. Draw symbols that represent your family on the assorted colors of paper. Then cut out the symbolic shapes.
2. Glue the symbols onto the 12" x 18" piece of black paper.
3. Use a black marker or crayon to make stitch marks around each symbol as shown.

Pride and Prejudice 💻
Understanding diversity, writing a bio poem

Black Americans have faced prejudice since the first Africans reached America in the early 1600s. Help students understand that prejudices can be overcome. Read aloud the story "The Sneetches" from *The Sneetches and Other Stories* by Dr. Seuss. Then have students discuss how the views of the two groups of Sneetches change after the stars keep getting mixed up and McBean leaves with his peculiar machine.

Create a bulletin board that celebrates diversity. Give each student a 4" x 6" index card and these instructions for writing an eight-line Bio Poem.

    Line 1: Write your first name.
    Line 2: Write three adjectives that describe you.
    Line 3: Write three things that you like.
    Line 4: Write three things that you fear or dislike.
    Line 5: Write the names of your siblings (or of your pets or friends if you have no siblings).
    Line 6: Write the names of your parents.
    Line 7: Write the name of the town in which you were born.
    Line 8: Write your last name.

Photograph each student as she writes her poem. Then post each Bio Poem with the appropriate photograph on a board under the title "Celebrate Diversity."

Bio Poem

Mitzi
Creative, Fun, Kind
Loves chocolate, movies, and reading
Fears mean dogs, storms, and collard greens
Siblings: Doug, Vickie, and Darla
Parents: Evelyn and Douglas
Born in Durham, North Carolina
Knight

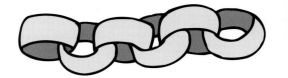

Chain of Events

- Abraham Lincoln issues the Emancipation Proclamation.
- Rosa Parks is arrested and the Civil Rights movement formally begins.
- The Fugitive Slave Act is passed.
- The Voting Rights Act is passed.

- The *Dred Scott* Supreme Court case states that slaves are property, not people.
- The armed forces become desegregated.
- Lyndon B. Johnson signs the Civil Rights Act.
- The term *underground railroad* is first used.

- The 15th Amendment is added to the Constitution.
- Martin Luther King Jr. leads more than 200,000 people in a protest march in Washington, D.C.
- The first African indentured servants arrive in the English colony of Jamestown, Virginia.
- The 13th Amendment is added to the Constitution.

- The Missouri Compromise divides states into free and slave.
- Jackie Robinson joins the Brooklyn Dodgers.
- Harriet Beecher Stowe writes *Uncle Tom's Cabin.*
- The *Brown v. the Board of Education* Supreme Court decision overturns the "separate but equal" ruling of 1896.

- Crispus Attucks is shot and killed during the Boston Massacre.
- Martin Luther King Jr. Day is declared a federal holiday.
- Peter Salem, Salem Poor, and other blacks fight at Bunker Hill.
- The 14th Amendment is added to the Constitution.

- Benjamin Banneker builds the first clock in America.
- The Civil War begins.
- The *Plessy v. Ferguson* Supreme Court decision declares that facilities for blacks be "separate but equal."
- Martin Luther King Jr. wins the Nobel Peace Prize.

- Massachusetts becomes the first colony to legalize slavery.
- The NAACP is founded.
- Jesse Jackson is a candidate for the Democratic presidential nomination.
- Martin Luther King Jr. is assassinated.

- Booker T. Washington opens Tuskegee Institute.
- Sojourner Truth becomes free after a law is passed in New York banning slavery.
- Jean Baptiste Pointe du Sable establishes a settlement that is to become Chicago.
- The slave ship *Amistad* is taken over by its African captives.

Note to the teacher: Duplicate one copy of this page to use with "Chain of Events" on page 26. Cut the eight fact
30 strips apart.

On the Road to Freedom

Increase your vocabulary and black history knowledge. Use the vocabulary words in the box to complete five of the ten activities described below. Put a check in the box beside each activity you complete.

race	civil rights
ethnic pride	abolitionist
culture	prejudice
segregation	oppression
integration	brotherhood
minority	self-determination
unity	nonviolence
discrimination	Underground Railroad

Vocabulary Activities

☐ 1. Write a definition for each vocabulary word. Do not use a form of the word in the definition.

☐ 2. Draw a picture to illustrate each word. Then write a sentence explaining each illustration.

☐ 3. Use each word in a sentence that also includes the name of a famous Black American.

☐ 4. Use as many of the words as you can in a paragraph about an important event in black history. Underline the vocabulary words used in the paragraph.

☐ 5. Develop ten questions related to black history using a vocabulary word in each question. Also provide the answers to the questions.

☐ 6. Make up ten questions for each of which a vocabulary word is the answer.

☐ 7. Write a black history rap or poem using as many of the vocabulary words as possible.

☐ 8. Create a crossword puzzle on graph paper using all the vocabulary words. Include the answer key on the back.

☐ 9. Construct a rebus puzzle (using letters and pictures) for each vocabulary word.

☐ 10. Make a concentration game by writing each vocabulary word on an index card and each definition on an index card. Play with a partner to see who can find the most matches when the cards are placed facedown.

Black American Achievers Contract

Select one person from the "Gallery of Black American Achievers" handout (page 33). Then find out more about that person by completing five of the ten activities described below. Check the box next to each activity that you complete. Be prepared to share two of your five completed activities with the class.

☐ 1. Develop ten questions you would ask if you could meet and interview your subject. Avoid yes/no questions.

☐ 2. Make a timeline of your subject's life. Include at least ten events on the timeline.

☐ 3. Select someone that you think your subject would consider a hero. Explain why.

☐ 4. Create a poster about your subject. Include biographical information, accomplishments, and pictures.

☐ 5. Create an acrostic poem about your subject. Write his or her full name vertically in all uppercase letters. Then think of an adjective or phrase that describes your subject and begins with each letter in his or her name. Write each adjective or phrase horizontally beside the appropriate letter.
      Example: **H**elped runaway slaves
                      A woman called Moses
                      Railroad
                      Risked her life
                      Inspirational
                      Escaped to freedom
                      Triumphant

☐ 6. Design a special award honoring your subject for an important achievement or accomplishment. Describe the award; then create a certificate, medal, or trophy labeled with the appropriate information.

☐ 7. If your subject had a motto, what would it be? Explain your reasons.

☐ 8. Create a political cartoon showing one of your subject's accomplishments. Write a brief explanation of the cartoon underneath your illustration.

☐ 9. Make a word find using ten adjectives that describe your subject. Underneath your puzzle, use each of the hidden adjectives in a sentence describing your subject.

☐ 10. If your subject is a historical figure, describe how you think he or she would react to the changes of modern society. If your subject is a modern figure, describe what you think his or her contributions to society may have been had he or she lived 100 years ago.

©The Education Center • *FEBRUARY* • TEC207

32 **Note to the teacher:** Use with "Black History Contracts" on page 23.

Gallery of Black American Achievers

The following list represents just a few of the many Black Americans who have made accomplishments in the fields and professions listed below.

Astronauts/Explorers
- Ronald McNair
- Guion Bluford
- Mae Carol Jemison
- Frederick Drew Gregory
- Matthew Henson
- James Pierson Beckwourth

Civil Rights Leaders
- Rosa Lee Parks
- Fannie Lou Hamer
- Coretta Scott King
- Dr. Martin Luther King Jr.
- Jesse Jackson
- W. E. B. Du Bois

Athletes
- Jesse Owens
- Jackie Robinson
- Arthur Ashe
- Wilma Rudolph
- Althea Gibson
- Jackie Joyner-Kersee

Singers
- Marian Anderson
- Leontyne Price
- Ella Fitzgerald
- Lena Horne
- Sarah Vaughan
- Nat "King" Cole

Writers
- Virginia Hamilton
- Alice Walker
- Toni Morrison
- Alex Haley
- Julius Lester
- Langston Hughes

Poets/Playwrights
- Phillis Wheatley
- Maya Angelou
- Gwendolyn Brooks
- Paul Laurence Dunbar
- Lorraine Hansberry

Government Officials
- Shirley Chisholm
- Ralph Bunche
- Barbara C. Jordan
- Thurgood Marshall
- Thomas Bradley
- Andrew Jackson Young Jr.

Educators
- Mary McLeod Bethune
- Booker T. Washington
- Benjamin E. Mays
- E. Franklin Frazier

Scientists/Inventors
- Ernest Everett Just
- Benjamin Banneker
- George W. Carver
- Garrett Morgan
- Jan Ernst Matzeliger
- Lewis Howard Latimer

Doctors/Nurses
- Charles Richard Drew
- Daniel Hale Williams
- Susie King Taylor
- Mary Elizabeth Mahoney

Musicians
- Louis Armstrong
- Count Basie
- Dean Dixon
- Duke Ellington
- Dizzy Gillespie
- Charlie Parker

Film/T.V. Personalities
- Sidney Poitier
- Bill Cosby
- Oprah Winfrey
- Louis Gossett Jr.
- Spike Lee
- James Earl Jones

Note to the teacher: Use with "Black History Contracts" on page 23 and "African American Achievers' Hall of Fame" on page 27.

African American Achievers' HALL OF FAME

_____
(Name)

_____
(Field or Profession)

Birthdate: _____   **Birthplace:** _____

Childhood/Family

Major Accomplishments

Illustration of an Important Accomplishment

Why This Person Should Be in the Hall of Fame

Name _____ *Cause and effect*

Causes & Effects in Black History

Match each cause to its effect by writing the letter of each effect in the box by its cause.

Causes

☐ Rosa Parks refuses to give up her seat to a white person.

☐ Public city school districts are ordered to desegregate schools.

☐ Jackie Robinson joins the Brooklyn Dodgers baseball team.

☐ The 13th Amendment to the Constitution is passed in 1865.

☐ Harriet Beecher Stowe's book *Uncle Tom's Cabin* is published.

☐ Abraham Lincoln signs the Emancipation Proclamation in 1863.

☐ Three police officers are found *not guilty* of all charges pertaining to the Rodney King beating.

☐ The Underground Railroad is organized.

☐ George Washington Carver writes and teaches about soil conservation and how to improve crop production.

☐ The triangle trade route is established.

Effects

A. Riots break out in Los Angeles.

B. Thousands of southern slaves escape slavery and gain freedom.

C. The Montgomery bus boycott begins.

D. Thousands of Africans are brought to North America.

E. Southern farmers learn how to be more productive.

F. Major-league professional sports become integrated.

G. Slavery is constitutionally abolished in the United States.

H. Slavery is made illegal in the Confederate States.

I. The argument over slavery becomes more intense.

J. Both black and white students are bused to schools outside their neighborhoods.

Bonus Box: On the back of this paper, write down two positive things you've done this year and their effects.

©The Education Center • *FEBRUARY* • TEC207 • Key p. 93 35

Gung-Hey-Fat-Choy!

(Happy New Year!)

Out with the old and in with the new! Capture the New Year spirit by celebrating Chinese New Year. This festival, with its ancient customs and traditions, takes place between mid-January and mid-February. Welcome the sights, sounds, and tastes of Chinese New Year with the following activities.

by Thad H. McLaurin

Predicting Your Future
Experiencing a cultural tradition, making a personal connection

What do a rooster, a snake, a rat, and a dragon have in common? Each animal represents one year in the 12-year cycle of the Chinese calendar. Other animals in this cycle include the monkey, sheep, horse, rabbit, tiger, ox, boar, and dog. Each animal represents a unique set of personality traits. According to Chinese folklore, a person has the same personality traits as the animal of the year under which he was born. It is traditional for a Chinese fortune-teller to use the year of birth to determine a baby's destiny. Under which years were your students born? Help them find out by creating this bulletin board. Enlarge and duplicate the round calendar pattern from page 39 onto yellow paper. Post it on red background paper under the title. Then decorate the board using one or more of the following ideas:

- Have each student use the dates on the pattern to find the animal for his birth year. Then make a chart for each year in which your students were born. Instruct each student to write his name on the appropriate chart.
- Duplicate page 40 for each student. Have the student locate the year in which he was born and then read his horoscope. Ask volunteers to share whether they agree or disagree with their horoscopes. Next have each student take home page 40 and complete the chart and the writing activity. The following day, have each student share the results of his chart. Use the results to graph the number of family members that do and do not match their horoscopes. Finally have the class evaluate the accuracy of the Chinese horoscope.
- Have select students share their paragraphs from the writing activity on page 40; then post each student's paragraph on the "Gung-Hey-Fat-Choy" bulletin board.

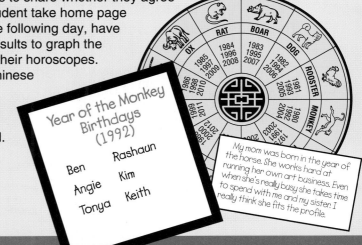

Year of the Monkey Birthdays (1992)

Ben   Rashaun
Angie   Kim
Tonya   Keith

My mom was born in the year of the horse. She works hard at running her own art business. Even when she's really busy she takes time to spend with me and my sister. I really think she fits the profile.

The Kitchen God
Experiencing a cultural tradition

The Chinese believe that Tsao-Chun, the Chinese kitchen god, watches over each family throughout the year. During Chinese New Year, he ascends to heaven and gives a report on each family. To ensure a good report, the home is cleaned thoroughly the month before the New Year begins, and red paper signs with good-luck messages and symbols are placed throughout the house. Fill your classroom with the smells of Chinese New Year by creating this traditional recipe.

Wontons

Ingredients/Supplies:

1 1/2 cups finely chopped
   cooked chicken (or one 13-ounce can)
2 tbsp. finely chopped celery
1 tbsp. soy sauce
1 wonton skin per student (available in the
   produce section of most supermarkets)
cooking oil

paper towels
mixing bowl
waxed paper
bowl of water
teaspoon
frying pan

STEP 3
STEP 4
STEP 5
STEP 6

Directions:

1. Combine the chicken, celery, and soy sauce in a bowl.
2. Place one wonton skin on a waxed-paper square for each student.
3. Put a rounded teaspoon of the chicken mixture in the center of each wonton skin.
4. Dip your index finder in water; then wet the edges of the wonton. Fold the wonton in half diagonally and seal the seams, creating a triangular pouch.
5. Pull the bottom corners toward each other.
6. Overlap the tips of the two bottom corners and pinch together.
7. Fry each wonton in about a half inch of cooking oil until light brown. Drain the wontons on paper towels and let them cool. Makes approximately 33 wontons.

Serve the wontons with warm tea. Challenge each student to eat his wonton using chopsticks (ask a local Chinese restaurant to donate some). Have students follow the directions below for using chopsticks.

How to Hold Chopsticks:

Step 1: Place the lower chopstick in the crook of your thumb beside the ring finger. This chopstick should remain still.

Step 2: Place the upper chopstick under your index finger and between your thumb and middle finger. This is similar to holding a pencil when writing. This chopstick will be moved up and down.

Step 3: Keep the lower chopstick still and move the upper chopstick to pick up your food.

Lighting the Way for a New Year 💻
Experiencing a cultural tradition, following directions

Chinese New Year always ends with the Lantern Festival. Children wear new clothes and people parade through the streets with illuminated lanterns of all shapes and sizes. As part of your celebration, have each student create his own Chinese lantern. Duplicate page 41 for each student. In addition have the student choose one 12" x 18" sheet and one 1" x 8" strip of red, yellow, black, or green paper.

Student directions for making a Chinese lantern:
1. Decorate the symbols on page 41 with markers and glitter.
2. Cut out each symbol and glue it securely to one side of the paper.
3. Fold the paper lengthwise with the symbols on the outside.
4. Cut slits 1/4-inch apart along the folded edge, stopping about one inch from the open end (Step 4).
5. Unfold the paper and spread glue along the two short ends (Step 5). Bend the paper around and press the two short ends together until the glue dries.
6. Glue the 1" x 8" strip to the inside of the lantern's top opening to create a handle (Step 6).

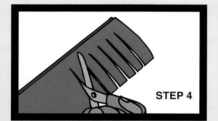

STEP 4

STEP 5

STEP 6

Luck and Lions 💻
Experiencing a cultural tradition, following directions

Lion dancers parade through the streets during the Lantern Festival. As dancers go from door-to-door, shopkeepers give them "Lucky Money" to ensure good fortune and to drive away bad luck for the new year.

Have each student create a Lion Dance mask by bringing in one paper grocery bag. Enlarge and duplicate the lion-mask pattern on page 39 for each student. Then duplicate page 41 for each student. Precut a supply of 48-inch-long yellow, blue, and green crepe-paper streamers. Instruct each student to select five streamers and then follow the directions below to create a lion mask.

Meanwhile ask parent volunteers to send in foil-wrapped, chocolate money and a red envelope for each student. Place several pieces of candy in each envelope to create "Lucky Money." Hide the envelopes around the room. Instruct each student to don his completed mask and then look for a "Lucky Money" envelope. After each student has found one envelope, let the students enjoy their treats.

Student directions for making a lion mask:
1. Paint the outside of your bag red. Let the paint dry.
2. Place the paper bag on your head. Roll up the bottom of the bag if it is too large. Then have a friend mark the location of your eyes using a marker.
3. Decorate the lion-mask pattern and the five Chinese symbols with glitter and markers.
4. Cut out the lion-mask pattern and the symbols. Cut eyeholes in the pattern.
5. Glue the pattern to the bag being sure to line up and cut slits for the eyeholes.
6. Glue the symbols to the sides and top of the paper bag.
7. Tape the streamers to the inside back of the mask.

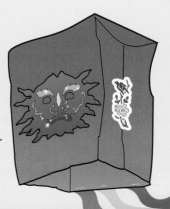

Use with "Luck and Lions" on page 38.

Chinese Zodiac

Use the Chinese zodiac below to see how well you really know your family. Write the name of each family member in the left-hand column of the chart below. In the middle column, write the birth year and the animal that matches that year. Finally place a check in the "Yes" column if the family member's personality matches the horoscope, or check the "No" column if it doesn't match the horoscope.

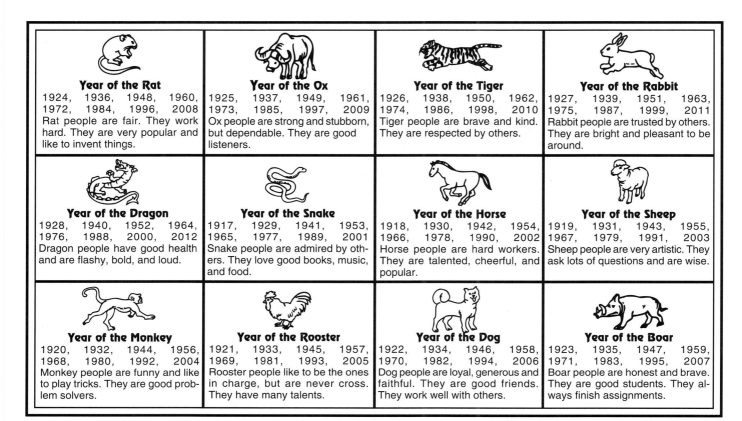

Year of the Rat
1924, 1936, 1948, 1960, 1972, 1984, 1996, 2008
Rat people are fair. They work hard. They are very popular and like to invent things.

Year of the Ox
1925, 1937, 1949, 1961, 1973, 1985, 1997, 2009
Ox people are strong and stubborn, but dependable. They are good listeners.

Year of the Tiger
1926, 1938, 1950, 1962, 1974, 1986, 1998, 2010
Tiger people are brave and kind. They are respected by others.

Year of the Rabbit
1927, 1939, 1951, 1963, 1975, 1987, 1999, 2011
Rabbit people are trusted by others. They are bright and pleasant to be around.

Year of the Dragon
1928, 1940, 1952, 1964, 1976, 1988, 2000, 2012
Dragon people have good health and are flashy, bold, and loud.

Year of the Snake
1917, 1929, 1941, 1953, 1965, 1977, 1989, 2001
Snake people are admired by others. They love good books, music, and food.

Year of the Horse
1918, 1930, 1942, 1954, 1966, 1978, 1990, 2002
Horse people are hard workers. They are talented, cheerful, and popular.

Year of the Sheep
1919, 1931, 1943, 1955, 1967, 1979, 1991, 2003
Sheep people are very artistic. They ask lots of questions and are wise.

Year of the Monkey
1920, 1932, 1944, 1956, 1968, 1980, 1992, 2004
Monkey people are funny and like to play tricks. They are good problem solvers.

Year of the Rooster
1921, 1933, 1945, 1957, 1969, 1981, 1993, 2005
Rooster people like to be the ones in charge, but are never cross. They have many talents.

Year of the Dog
1922, 1934, 1946, 1958, 1970, 1982, 1994, 2006
Dog people are loyal, generous and faithful. They are good friends. They work well with others.

Year of the Boar
1923, 1935, 1947, 1959, 1971, 1983, 1995, 2007
Boar people are honest and brave. They are good students. They always finish assignments.

Family Member	Birth Year & Animal	Matches Horoscope	
		Yes	**No**
(Example) Mom	1960—The Year of the Rat	✔	

Writing activity: Select one family member from the chart. On a 5" x 7" index card, write a paragraph explaining whether or not this person's personality fits that described in his or her zodiac profile. Give specific examples.

Note to the teacher: Use with "Predicting Your Future" on page 36. Provide each student with one 5" x 7" index card.

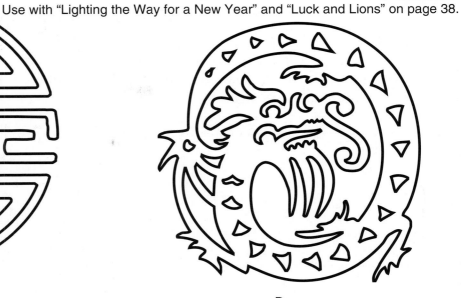

Long Life Symbol
This symbolizes the wish for a long life.

Dragon
The dragon symbolizes good luck.

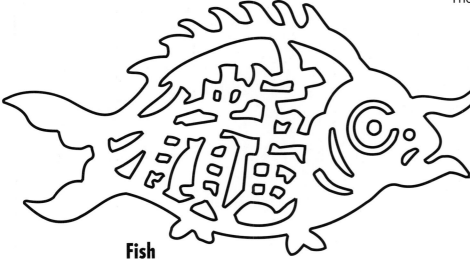

Fish
The fish symbolizes abundance or wealth.

Qilin
(CHEE-LIN)
This magical unicorn-like beast symbolizes goodness and a family with many children.

Plum Blossom
The plum blossom symbolizes virtue as well as the beginning of spring.

In a Pickle? Call on a Friend!

Follow up Valentine's Day with a celebration of International Friendship Week, held the last week of February. The following activities will inspire your students to form friendships and foster unity as they learn more about each other, their community, and the world.

by Chris Christensen and Thad McLaurin

Friends to the Rescue 🖥
Working cooperatively, problem solving

Don't throw out that pickle jar! Use it to encourage positive student interaction and improve problem-solving skills in your classroom. First thoroughly clean the inside of a large pickle jar. Keep the label on the outside intact. Then display the jar next to a shoebox that's been covered with green paper. Label the side of the box to read, "Help! I'm in a pickle!" Make ten copies of the three pickle patterns (page 49) on green paper; then cut them out. Place the pickle patterns in the box. Invite each student to fill out a pickle if she needs help with a school subject. Then have her place the pickle in the jar. Plan a time each day to empty the jar and pair each student who has requested help with a student who can provide the assistance.

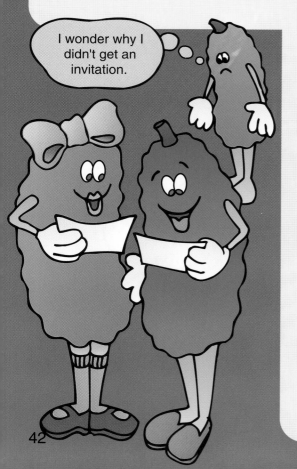

We're in a Pickle
Problem solving

Oops! Your best friend told you to call her and you forgot! Now you're really in a pickle. Use this scenario to explain this expression to your students. Then, in honor of Eat a Pickle Day (February 7), explore ways of getting out of "friendship pickles." Divide the class into groups of three or four. Each day during the week of February 7, present one of the problems listed below. Instruct each group to discuss possible solutions to the problem. Allow five minutes for discussion; then have each group present its solution. As an added attraction, serve a variety of pickles on one of the days for the students to munch on while problem solving.

- What would you do if your best friend blamed you for something you didn't do?
- What would you do if a friend had a party and didn't invite you?
- What would you do if you heard some really juicy gossip about a friend?
- What would you do if a new student who didn't speak English joined your class?
- What would you do if you had promised to help someone and then you forgot?

Friendship Booklets 🖥
Writing for a purpose

Spark student creativity and add a friendly touch to your classroom by having each student create a Friendship Booklet. Duplicate a class set of the "Friendship" pattern (page 49) onto yellow, orange, or red construction paper. Give each student one pattern to cut out; then instruct her to trace the pattern onto another sheet of colored paper to create a back cover. Next, have the student measure and cut four 5" x 7" sheets of white paper to be used as the inside pages of her booklet. Give each student a 12-inch length of yarn. Have the student use the directions below to construct her book. Instruct the student to illustrate pages 3–8.

Student directions:
Covers: Color and illustrate the front and back covers.
Page 1: Title page. Write a title and your name.
Page 2: Write a dedication. Also write the copyright date and publisher information.
Page 3: Complete this sentence: "A friend is someone who helps…"
Page 4: Complete this sentence: "A friend is someone who shows…"
Page 5: Complete this sentence: "A friend is someone who likes to…"
Page 6: Complete this sentence: "A friend is someone who always…"
Page 7: Complete this sentence: "A friend is someone who never…"
Page 8: Complete this sentence: "A friend is someone who knows…"

As each student completes her booklet, instruct her to arrange the pages in the correct order and then punch two holes in the left-hand side of the booklet. Next, direct her to use the yarn to bind the booklet by threading it through the holes and tying a bow on the front of the booklet.

Cover a bulletin board with blue paper. Create a large sun out of yellow paper as shown. Place the sun in the center of the board. Then post each booklet around the sun to create rays. Staple just the back cover of each booklet to the board so that each booklet can be read.

Hands Across the Classroom
Understanding the significance of a holiday

Kick off the celebration of International Friendship Week by having students create a "Hands Across the Classroom" garland. Duplicate one copy of the top pattern on page 50 for each male student and one copy of the bottom pattern for each female student. Instruct each student to write his or her name on the pattern and then add individual facial features and clothing. Direct each student to cut out his pattern.

Create a garland by lining up the patterns on a wall so that the hand of each pattern is touching another pattern. Expand the show of unity and friendship within your school by inviting other classes to help you create a school garland. Display the completed project in a main hallway for parents and visitors to enjoy.

Recipe for Friendship
Recognizing the qualities of friendship

Don your apron, gather up your mixing bowl, and don't forget the spoon! Have your students "cook up" the ingredients of a good friendship. Warm up to this activity by covering a cookbook with paper and labeling it "Recipes for a Friend." Then cover several cake-mix boxes and cans and label each with a quality of a good friendship, such as loyalty, honesty, patience, and sincerity. Display the cookbook, boxes, cans, several cooking utensils, and bowls at a "cooking station." Have your students gather around and, after allowing them to guess, explain that they are going to create a recipe for friendship. Show the boxes and cans labeled with the qualities of a good friendship. Ask students to name other qualities and list their responses on the board. Then divide the students into groups of three or four. Give each group one 3" x 5" index card. Instruct each group to determine how many cups of each friendship ingredient is needed to create a good friendship. Direct the group to write the amounts for each ingredient and the directions for making the recipe on the index card. Have each group present its recipe and explain why it felt more of some ingredients were needed than others.

"Ewe" Are Special
Recognizing contributions of others

Every school has employees, parents, and volunteers who do wonderful things for the students and teaching staff. Recognize the hard work of these individuals with a "Ewe" Are Special Day. Duplicate a class set of the award on page 51 onto white construction paper. Then ask each student to name a special helper in the school such as the school secretary, a custodian, the librarian, or a parent volunteer. List each helper's name next to the name of the student who suggested him. Pair no more than two students to the same special helper. Distribute one " 'Ewe' Are Special Award" to each student. Then instruct each student to fill out the award and decorate it. Schedule a "Ewe" Are Special Day so that students may present their awards to the recipients.

Seeds of Friendship
Creative thinking

Like a fertile seed, a new friendship grows strong under the right conditions. Make this point by having students brainstorm the steps to successfully growing a plant from a seed. Then have students compare this process to cultivating a new friendship. Point out that both seeds and friendships need nurturing in order to grow. Show students several seed packets. Duplicate the "Seeds of Friendship" pattern (page 51) for each student. Instruct each student to design his own "Seeds of Friendship" packet. First have him create an original slogan such as " 'Lettuce' Always Be Friends!" or "Thank You for 'Bean' My Friend!" Have him write and illustrate the slogan on his pattern. Direct each student to cut out his pattern and then fold and glue the two side tabs to the back of the package to create a pocket. Give each student a handful of inexpensive seeds to place inside his packet. After he folds and glues the top tab to the back of the package, invite each student to share his slogan with the rest of the class. Then encourage the student to present his package to a friend.

Friendship Webs
Recognizing the qualities of friendship

Recognizing the characteristics of a good friend helps students to establish stronger friendships. A ball of yarn is all you need to help your students acknowledge their classmates' positive qualities.

Sit the class in a large circle on the floor. Holding the end of a large ball of yarn in one hand, roll the ball to a student in the circle. As you roll the ball, state one positive quality about that student. When the student receives the ball, have him hold onto the yarn and roll the ball to another student in the circle. As he rolls, have him state a positive comment about that next student. Continue until a giant friendship web is spun around the circle. Afterward, have students reflect on the friendship web by asking them these questions: "Is the web strong?", "How is the web like a network of friends?", and "What is good about having more than one friend?"

Make a New Friend Day
Writing for a purpose, recognizing positive traits in others

Pair up with another teacher at your grade level to celebrate Make a New Friend Day. Match each student in your classroom with a student from your colleague's classroom. Then plan joint activities to last throughout the day. Begin the day by having each student write a friendly letter to introduce herself to her partner. Bring the two classes together. Have students swap letters and introduce themselves. Next, schedule a joint art, reading, or music activity. Plan a special luncheon for the two classes. In the afternoon plan a game for the students to play with their new friends. Wind up the day by having each student write a letter to her new friend describing what she enjoyed about the day and stating one positive comment about her new friend.

Under Pressure
Developing an understanding through discussion

Students often find themselves pushed or coaxed into uncomfortable situations. Invite the school counselor to come and discuss peer pressure and the effects it can have on a friendship. Have the counselor share strategies that the students can use today to avoid uncomfortable situations. In addition to the school counselor, invite local role models to share how they successfully handled difficult situations and still managed to make good friends while growing up. As a follow-up activity, ask the counselor to return in a month and have the students share the progress they have made using the strategies and suggestions given earlier.

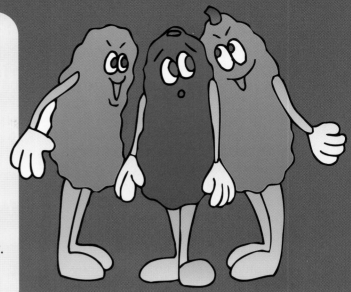

Cinquain Chums 💻
Recognizing positive traits in others, writing a cinquain poem

Bring out the poet in each student with the following interactive writing activity. Begin by having each student write her name on a slip of paper. Place each slip in a paper bag. Then have each student draw one name from the bag. Have each student write a cinquain about the person whose name she drew from the bag. Explain that a cinquain is a five-line poem and that each line describes a different quality about the subject. Have each student follow the cinquain format and directions below to write her poem.

Cinquain

Line 1: The student's name.
Line 2: Two adjectives that describe the student.
Line 3: Three verbs that tell something that the student enjoys doing.
Line 4: Another adjective that describes the student.
Line 5: A positive three-word description of the student.

Joe
patient, positive
runs, gardens, reads
intelligent
loves helping others

Next, divide the students into small groups. Provide each group with white glue and one cup of tempera paint. Give each student in the group one 5 1/2" x 8 1/2" sheet of white paper, one 8 1/2" x 11" sheet of colored paper, and one drinking straw. Have each student follow the directions below to present her cinquain. When students have completed their displays, collect the poems and mount them on a bulletin board. Then allow time for each student to find and read the cinquain that was written just for her.

Student directions:
1. Write the cinquain on the 5 1/2" x 8 1/2" sheet of white paper.
2. Use the glue to mount the cinquain on the colored sheet of paper.
3. Use the straw to drop a dab of paint onto the white paper.
4. Blow through the straw to create paint splatters across the paper.
5. Write your name on the back of the colored sheet of paper.

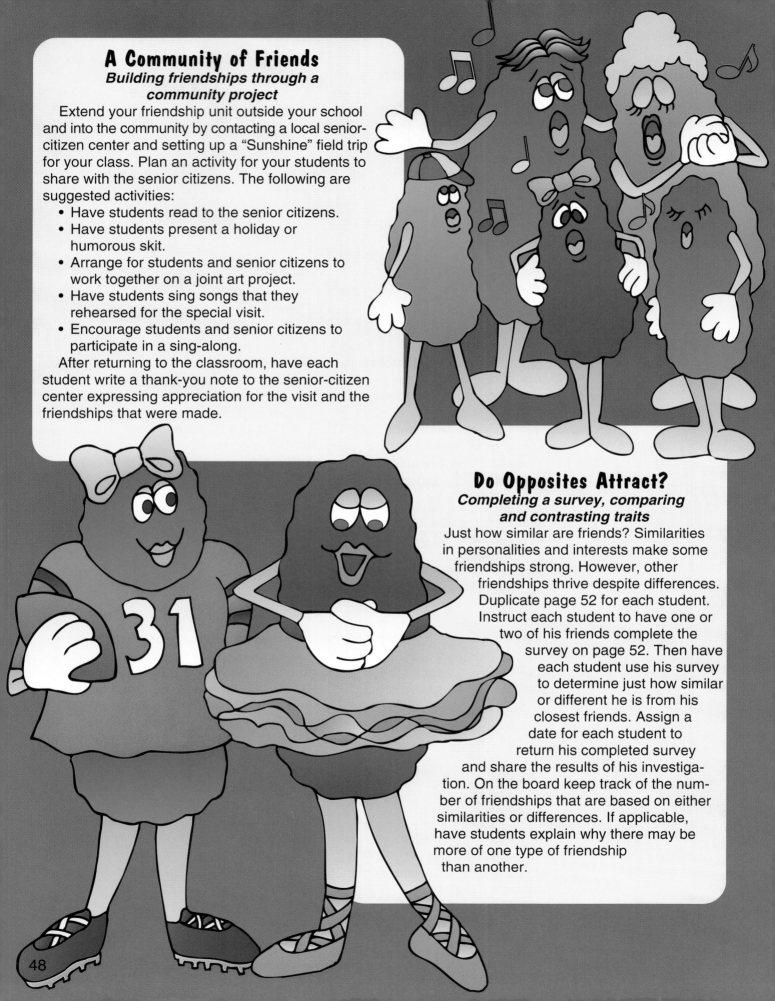

A Community of Friends
Building friendships through a community project

Extend your friendship unit outside your school and into the community by contacting a local senior-citizen center and setting up a "Sunshine" field trip for your class. Plan an activity for your students to share with the senior citizens. The following are suggested activities:

- Have students read to the senior citizens.
- Have students present a holiday or humorous skit.
- Arrange for students and senior citizens to work together on a joint art project.
- Have students sing songs that they rehearsed for the special visit.
- Encourage students and senior citizens to participate in a sing-along.

After returning to the classroom, have each student write a thank-you note to the senior-citizen center expressing appreciation for the visit and the friendships that were made.

Do Opposites Attract?
Completing a survey, comparing and contrasting traits

Just how similar are friends? Similarities in personalities and interests make some friendships strong. However, other friendships thrive despite differences. Duplicate page 52 for each student. Instruct each student to have one or two of his friends complete the survey on page 52. Then have each student use his survey to determine just how similar or different he is from his closest friends. Assign a date for each student to return his completed survey and share the results of his investigation. On the board keep track of the number of friendships that are based on either similarities or differences. If applicable, have students explain why there may be more of one type of friendship than another.

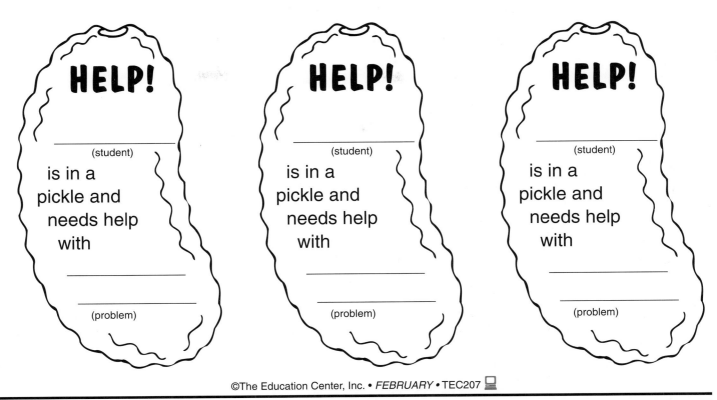

HELP!

_____
(student)

is in a
pickle and
needs help
with

_____

_____
(problem)

HELP!

_____
(student)

is in a
pickle and
needs help
with

_____

_____
(problem)

HELP!

_____
(student)

is in a
pickle and
needs help
with

_____

_____
(problem)

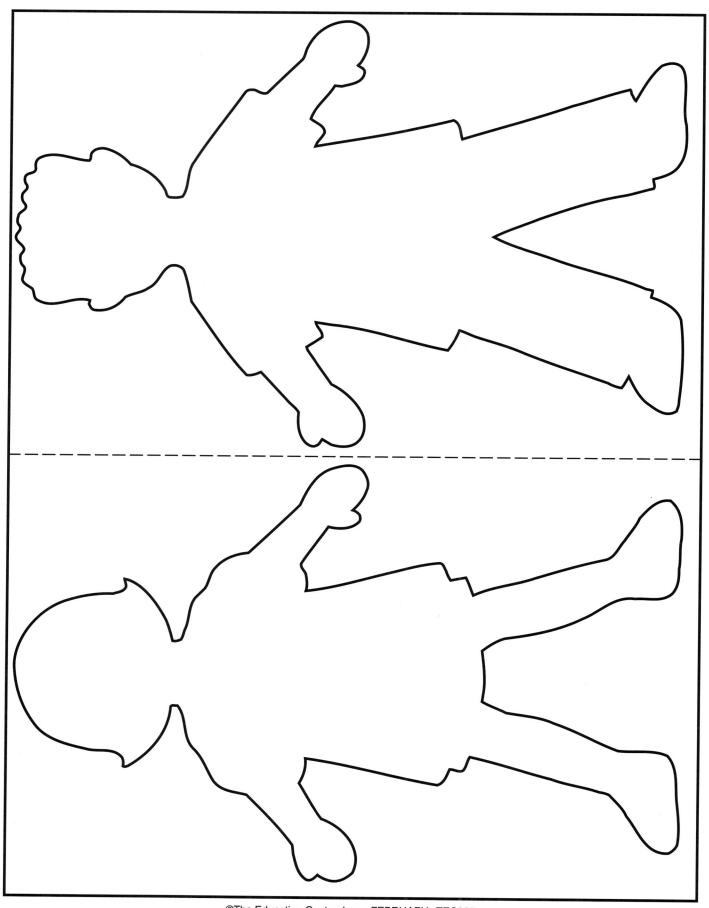

50 **Note to the teacher:** Use both patterns with "Hands Across the Classroom" on page 44. Duplicate one copy of the top pattern for each male student. Duplicate one copy of the bottom pattern for each female student.

"Ewe" Are Special Award

Presented to

_____

"Ewe" are special because...

_____

_____

©The Education Center, Inc. • *FEBRUARY* • TEC207

Use with "Seeds of Friendship" on page 45.

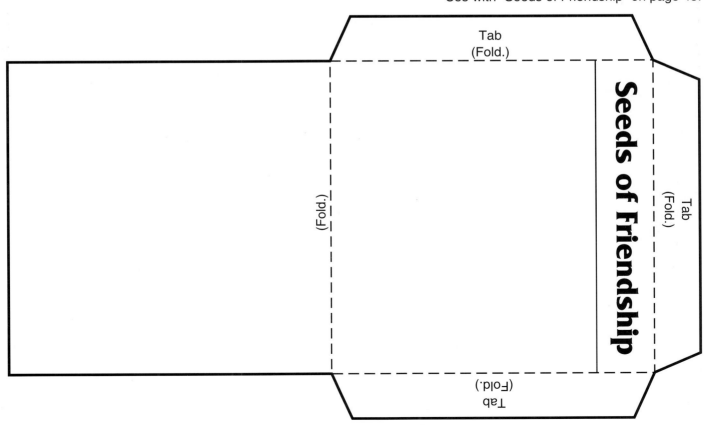

Tab
(Fold.)

(Fold.)

Seeds of Friendship

Tab
(Fold.)

Tab
(Fold.)

Do Opposites Attract?

Just how similar are you to your friends? Similar likes and dislikes make some friendships strong, while other friendships are strong despite differences. Use this survey to find out just how you are similar to or different from your closest friends.

Directions: Have one or two of your friends complete the survey below. Then complete the survey yourself.

	My friend _____ (name)	My friend _____ (name)	**Myself**
Favorite Food			
Favorite Dessert			
Favorite Color			
Favorite Game			
Favorite Movie			
Favorite Television Show			
Favorite Book			
Favorite Place			
Favorite Sport			
Favorite Song			
Favorite Singer			
Favorite School Subject			
Favorite Actor/Actress			
Favorite Pet			
Favorite Season			
Favorite Candy			

Analyze the Data

Are your friendships based on similarities or differences? In the space provided below, use the data collected in the survey to conclude why your friendships are strong.

_____

_____

_____

_____

_____

_____

Note to the teacher: Duplicate this page for each student to use with "Do Opposites Attract?" on page 48.

Name _____ *Contract*

A Friend in Need

Due Date:_____

Below are several opportunities for you to help a friend, make a friend, and read about friends. Choose at least three activities to complete by the due date. Put a check in the box in front of each activity you complete.

☐ Make a special card for a friend. Inside the card write a poem about your friendship. Decorate the cover with markers, crayons, and glitter.

☐ Write a letter to a friend and tell him about International Friendship Week. Inform him that it takes place the last week of February. In your letter tell your friend what you appreciate about your friendship.

☐ Make a list of the friendly deeds you do for a week. Include the name of each person or organization that you help and a brief description of each good deed.

☐ Read one of the following books about friendship. Write a brief summary of the novel, including the setting, plot, climax, and conclusion.

- *The Pinballs* by Betsy Byars
- *The Cay* by Theodore Taylor
- *Strider* by Beverly Cleary
- *Cousins* by Virginia Hamilton
- *Me, Mop and the Moondance Kid* by Walter Dean Myers

☐ Write a description of a favorite friend. Be sure to include the following:
- Your friend's full name.
- What your friend looks like.
- Three things you like about your friend.
- Two things your friend enjoys.
- An illustration of your friend.

☐ At lunchtime sit with someone new. Discuss your likes and dislikes. Afterwards summarize your conversation in a paragraph. Be sure to include the name of the person you sat with and any new information you learned about that person.

☐ Be a homework helper. Help a fellow classmate complete a homework assignment that is giving her difficulty. Record the name of the student you help, the homework assignment, the date, and the amount of time you spend helping the student.

☐ Create a poster showing the qualities that you feel make a good friend. Use markers, magazine clippings, and original art to create the poster.

☐ Write about a time when a friend did something special for you. Include the name of the friend, a description of the good deed, and how it made you feel.

Note to the teacher: Duplicate this page for each student. Assign a due date. Have each student share at least one completed activity with his classmates.

Hail to the Chief!

Thematic Activities for Learning About the Presidents

Step into the Oval Office for an inside look at the presidency. As you celebrate the births of Lincoln and Washington, use the following activities to enrich your students' knowledge of the more than 40 men who have been called "Mr. President."

by Thad H. McLaurin and Elizabeth Lindsay

Executive States 🖳
Data collecting and graphing

Can your state boast as the birthplace of a president? Help students find out by dividing the class into ten groups. Assign each group four or five different presidents. Instruct each group to research the birthplaces of its presidents and share its findings. Tally the results on the board as each group presents its data. Then have students help you compile the data into a class graph. List the states on the vertical axis and the number of presidents on the horizontal axis.

Arkansas—William J. Clinton
California—Richard M. Nixon
Connecticut—George W. Bush
Georgia—James E. Carter
Illinois—Ronald Reagan
Iowa—Herbert Hoover
Kentucky—Abraham Lincoln
Massachusetts—John Adams, John Quincy Adams, John F. Kennedy, George Bush
Missouri—Harry S. Truman
Nebraska—Gerald Ford

New Hampshire—Franklin Pierce
New Jersey—Grover Cleveland
New York—Martin Van Buren, Millard Fillmore, Theodore Roosevelt, Franklin D. Roosevelt
North Carolina—James K. Polk, Andrew Johnson
Ohio—Ulysses S. Grant, Rutherford B. Hayes, James Garfield, Benjamin Harrison, William McKinley, William H. Taft, Warren G. Harding

Pennsylvania—James Buchanan
South Carolina—Andrew Jackson
Texas—Dwight D. Eisenhower, Lyndon Johnson
Vermont—Chester A. Arthur, Calvin Coolidge
Virginia—George Washington, Thomas Jefferson, James Madison, James Monroe, William Henry Harrison, John Tyler, Zachary Taylor, Woodrow Wilson

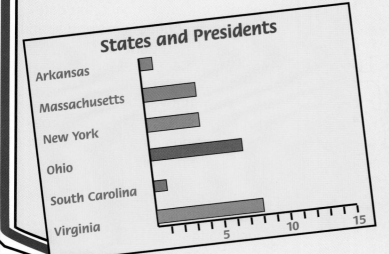

States and Presidents

"Presidential Rap"
Understanding the importance of individuals through song

Help students learn some simple facts about the presidents by introducing the "Presidential Rap" on page 62. Make one copy of the rap for each student. Rehearse the rap a few minutes each day during the week before Presidents' Day. Then, on Presidents' Day, invite other classes and parents to a special performance of the Presidential Rap. If a new president has been recently elected, have your students create a new verse to add to the end of the rap.

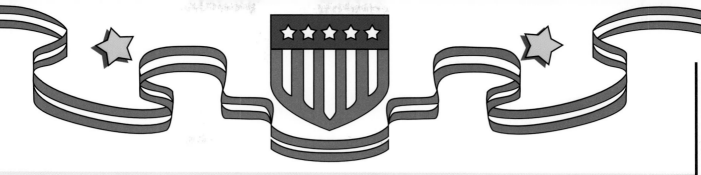

Virginia's Pride 💻

Mapping, developing an understanding through discussion

What do Presidents Washington, Jefferson, Madison, Monroe, W. H. Harrison, Tyler, Taylor, and Wilson have in common? They were all born in Virginia, of course. Map out the presidential birthplaces using the data collected in the "Executive States" activity on page 54. Cover a bulletin board with a large U.S. map. Give each student the names of one or two presidents and a slip of 2" x 3" red paper for each one. Instruct the student to write the name of a president on each slip. Then have him staple each slip to the board near that president's birth state. Direct each student to use string and map pins to connect each slip to its corresponding state. When students have completed this display, have them discuss answers to questions such as the following: Why do some states, such as Virginia, have more presidents than others? Why do many states have no presidents? Why do you think our state does/doesn't have a president?

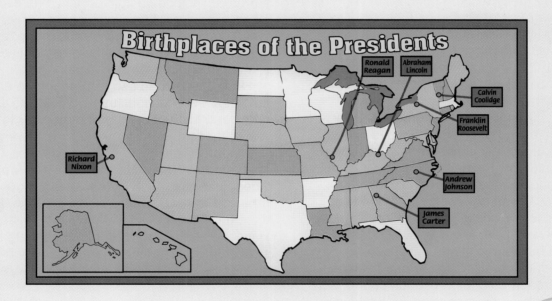

Thomas Jefferson: Jack of All Trades

Creative thinking, writing for a purpose

Thomas Jefferson did more than write the Declaration of Independence. He studied many different subjects, such as mathematics, law, botany, music, architecture, farming, and archaeology. Jefferson also enjoyed inventing gadgets to help improve everyday life. His creations included a quartet book stand, a more efficient plow, and a polygraph machine. Some of Jefferson's gadgets were improvements on existing items, such as his swivel chair.

Let Thomas Jefferson inspire your students to create new or improved gadgets. Divide students into pairs. Direct each pair to think up and illustrate an invented or improved gadget. Then instruct each pair to write a paragraph explaining how its creation will improve everyday life. Have each pair tell the class about its gadget. Then display the illustrations and paragraphs around the classroom.

Farmer George?
Observing and collecting data, critical thinking

We usually remember presidents for their accomplishments in office. However, many led interesting lives before and after their terms as president. George Washington was a very successful farmer. He experimented to find crops that were as profitable as tobacco. The following activity is similar to studies Washington conducted with wheat, corn, oats, and barley.

Purchase four inexpensive paint buckets and poke drainage holes in the bottom of each one. Get permission to fill each bucket with soil samples from your school grounds. Pour the soil from all four buckets into a pile on the ground. Break up any lumps, remove weeds and rocks, and mix the soil thoroughly. Return the soil to each bucket. Label one bucket "wheat," one "corn," one "oats," and one "barley." Plant ten wheat, corn, oat, and barley seeds in the appropriate buckets. Keep the soil in each bucket moist and in full sun. Divide students into pairs. Make one copy of page 63 for each pair. Instruct each pair to observe the plants daily and record its observations on the "Farmer George's Data Chart." As the plants mature, have each pair use its observations and data chart to evaluate each plant. Then have each pair conclude which plant or plants would best grow in the soil near the classroom. Record the conclusions on the board. Then have the class compare its findings to George Washington's findings. (He made corn and wheat his main crops.) Invite students to explain why their results are similar to or different from Washington's.

Interview With Mr. President: Take One
Researching a topic, role playing

Daily television news programs help students become more familiar with political personalities. Take advantage of this forum by having your students create mock interviews of past or present presidents. Divide the class into groups of three. Assign each group one president and instruct the group to gather biographical information about the president's life before he came into office. Have the group include such information as his birthplace, birth date, family history, and other important facts. In addition, have each group research something important that the president accomplished during his term in office.

Have each group use its research to develop ten interview questions that it would like to ask its president. Instruct each group member to select one of the following roles: the *interviewer*, the *president*, or the *video camera operator*. Direct each group to use its ten questions to prepare a video interview. Allow time for each group to rehearse and videotape its presentation. Remind each group to check for proper lighting and sound. Have the audience monitor the speakers to make sure they can be clearly heard. Then schedule a day for the groups to present their interviews.

Motto Madness 💻

Writing for a purpose

Presidential candidates often use catchy mottoes or slogans to express their beliefs, goals, ideals, and promises. Ask students to name the various places that candidates have displayed such mottoes, such as on bumper stickers, buttons, and posters. Share some of the mottoes used in past elections (see the list below), and invite students to discuss the meanings of these sayings.

Create some original mottoes by having your students brainstorm topics that are important to a successful classroom. Include on that list such qualities as honesty, respect, hard work, ingenuity, and determination. Then instruct each student to create a motto for his classroom. Give each student a 5" x 12" piece of white poster board. Tell the student to make a bumper sticker using his original classroom motto. Encourage each student to use bold colors and graphics. Display the bumper stickers on a bulletin board titled "Motto Madness." If you have access to a button maker, extend the activity by having students create buttons for their mottoes.

⭐ Don't Swap Horses Lincoln for President! ⭐

More Presidential Mottoes

"Tippecanoe and Tyler, too."—William Henry Harrison
"It is not best to swap horses while crossing the river."—Abraham Lincoln
"Let us have peace."—Ulysses S. Grant
"He kept us out of war."—Woodrow Wilson
"Keep cool with Coolidge."—Calvin Coolidge
"The buck stops here."—Harry S. Truman
"I like Ike."—Dwight D. Eisenhower

Campaign Speeches

Researching a topic, writing for a purpose

Did you know that Franklin Delano Roosevelt was the first president to be televised? And that Warren G. Harding was the first president to speak over the radio? Before the invention of radio and television, presidential candidates found it challenging to make their views and beliefs known to the voters. Candidates had to travel all over the country giving campaign speeches and talking with the people. Newspapers often printed the speeches for the public to read.

Use the following activity to enrich your students' knowledge of past presidential elections. Divide the class into groups of two or three. Have each group select a past presidential campaign to research, looking closely for the issues of that election year. Next, have the group use its research to write a campaign speech for one of the candidates based on those issues. As each group presents its speech, invite the audience to listen for and identify the issues, as well as the candidate's point of view on those issues.

Dinner at the White House
Experiencing a tradition

Have you ever wondered what the president and his family eat for dinner? Astound your students with the following favorite foods of some of the presidents:

- Cream of peanut soup and Virginia spoon bread were favorites of George Washington.
- Ulysses S. Grant ate a cucumber soaked in vinegar for breakfast.
- Corned beef and cabbage were at the top of Grover Cleveland's dining list.
- Dwight D. Eisenhower's favorite dessert was prune whip.
- Fettucini was a favorite of John F. Kennedy.
- Lyndon Johnson had many favorites including chili, corn pudding, and pecan pie.
- Cottage cheese covered with ketchup was a favorite lunch of Richard Nixon.
- George Bush enjoyed Tex-Mex chili and Chinese take-out food.

Below are two recipes for a simple meal enjoyed by George and Martha Washington. Recruit parent volunteers to prepare these dishes for your class to sample. Bon appétit!

Cream of Peanut Soup

Ingredients:

2 quarts canned chicken broth
2 onions, peeled and chopped
4 carrots, chopped
2 cups creamy peanut butter

2 cups half-and-half
1 cup dry-roasted peanuts, shelled
2 dashes salt and pepper
2 dashes hot sauce

Directions:

Place the chicken broth, onions, and carrots into a large soup pot. Bring to a boil; then cover and lower the heat to simmer. Cook until the carrots and onions are soft. Pour the mixture into a blender and puree. Return the mixture to the pot and add the remaining ingredients. Bring to a simmer and serve. Serves 12.

Virginia Spoon Bread

Ingredients:

1 cup cornmeal
1 1/2 teaspoons salt
2 cups milk

2 1/2 teaspoons baking powder
2 eggs, beaten

Directions:

Heat the milk so that it is very hot, but not boiling. Stir in the cornmeal and salt. Cook over low heat until the mixture is smooth and thick, stirring all the time. Continue to cook for about ten minutes, stirring occasionally. Remove from the heat to cool slightly. Add the baking powder and eggs. Mix thoroughly. Pour the mixture into a greased 8" square pan. Bake at 375°F for 30–35 minutes. Serves 8. Serve the cornbread with a spoon.

Scavenger Hunt Scrapbook
Researching a topic, acknowledging contributions in history

Capture the essence of each president by creating a Scavenger Hunt Scrapbook. Stock the following items at a center in your classroom: 9" x 12" colored paper, glue, scissors, crayons, markers, and old magazines. Assign each student a different president. Instruct her to research that president's characteristics and accomplishments. Then have her use that information to create a one-page collage (front and back) for the scrapbook. Tell her to scavenge through the magazines for items that represent characteristics and accomplishments of her president. Encourage each student to add photocopies from other sources as well as original artwork. Instruct her to mount the collected items and original artwork on a sheet of paper. Enlist a group of students to create a cover and a back for the scrapbook. Punch holes in the left margin of each page using a three-hole punch. Then use yarn or brads to bind the scrapbook. Display the book in the classroom or library. Or send it home each night with a different student to share with her parents.

Televised Debates
Critical thinking

The 1960 presidential campaign was the first in which the two candidates debated on national television and could be seen by millions of viewers at once. Have students explain how this televised debate made the 1960 presidential campaign different from campaigns of the past. Then ask students what effect this may have had on the outcome of the election. Finally, have students share other methods that modern presidential candidates use to spread their values and beliefs all over the country.

Picturing the Perfect President
Critical thinking

According to the Constitution, the requirements for the United States presidency are as follows: (1) you must be a natural-born citizen of the United States; (2) you must be at least 35 years old; and (3) you must have been a U.S. resident for at least 14 years. Seems rather easy, right? Well, whoever is elected president will have many national and international issues to face. Have students brainstorm a list of issues, such as crime and drug abuse, that face the president. Have students list other requirements they think a candidate should have to equip him or her to face these issues (examples include knowledge, experience, communication skills, and integrity). Divide the students into small groups. Have each group choose a different issue from the first list. Then have the group select from the second list the presidential characteristics most likely to help a president deal with this issue. Finally, have each group share its findings with the rest of the class.

The First Ladies

Researching a topic, comparing and contrasting information

From the 1700s to the present, America's first ladies have played a variety of roles as partners to the presidents. Help students understand how the first lady's role has changed over the past 200 years. Assign each student one first lady to research. (Make sure that a student researches the current first lady.) Have the student find information about the first lady's social and political duties, attitudes, and roles. Draw a Venn diagram on the board. In the left circle, list the duties, attitudes, and roles common only to early first ladies (see the diagram). In the right circle, list those items common only to the most recent first lady. Finally, list those items that are common to all first ladies in the intersecting section of the circles. Remind students of how changes in transportation and communication have affected the first lady's position and influence. Have students discuss why they think certain duties and responsibilities have not changed over the years. Finally, present these questions to the class: What qualities would the first female president's *husband* need to have? What would his title be?

First Ladies of the 18th and 19th Centuries

The Current First Lady

(Differences) (Similarities) (Differences)

Talking Tales

Researching a topic, participating in an oral presentation

Pair public speaking with basic biography to create a presidential Book Talk—a short, five-minute oral presentation with visuals. Instruct each student to read a presidential biography. Duplicate page 64 for each student. Instruct each student to gather information about the birthdate, birthplace, childhood, family, education, and accomplishments of his president using the "Book Talk Map." Allow the student to use his completed map as a cue card during his presentation. In addition, instruct each student to create a visual display to accompany his presentation. The visual may be a poster, model, *realia* box (a box of collected items), video, or diorama. Or suggest that the student present his Book Talk as if he were that president talking about his own life. If desired, videotape each Book Talk presentation and play it back so that the student can critique himself.

Fitness and Fun
Researching a topic

Many presidents have been sports enthusiasts. Ronald Reagan was a lifeguard in his youth and also enjoyed horseback riding. Jimmy Carter and Bill Clinton enjoyed jogging. John Kennedy played touch football while in office. Have students research the other sports interests of presidents. Give each student a copy of page 65. Challenge her to find at least one president for each sport listed on the page. After each student has completed the page, discuss why some sports, such as fishing, hunting, and horseback riding, have been more popular than other sports.

Trivia Trek
Building on background knowledge

Did you know George Washington wore false teeth made out of cow's teeth, lead, hippopotamus teeth, elephant and walrus tusks, and human teeth? Take a closer look at the quirky side of the presidency by playing "Race for the White House" (pages 66 and 67). Provide reference books and other materials for students to use during the game. Duplicate the directions below. Mount the directions, the gameboard, and the Trivia Card on colored paper and laminate all three for durability. Store the three items in an envelope labeled with the game's title. Invite students to play the game during free time or as a center activity.

"Race for the White House"

Number of players: 3
Supplies needed: 1 die, 2 game pieces, gameboard (page 66), Trivia Card (page 67)

Directions:
1. Pick two people to be players and one person to be the Trivia Card holder.
2. Each player rolls the die to see who goes first.
3. In turn each player rolls the die and moves that number of spaces.
4. If a player lands on a square with an interesting fact, he reads the fact, then moves ahead three spaces.
5. If a player lands on a space with a direction, he follows the direction.
6. If a player lands on a Trivia Card square, the Trivia Card holder asks the player a question from the Trivia Card. If the player answers correctly, he moves ahead five spaces. If he answers incorrectly, he moves back three spaces.
7. Players may use reference books and materials to help them answer the Trivia Card questions.
8. The first player to reach the White House wins the game.
9. The winner of the game plays the Trivia Card holder in the next game. The loser becomes the new Trivia Card holder.

George Washington was 57 years old when he became toothless!

Presidential Rap

U.S. presidents have a tough job, you see;
They've faced many challenges, more than you and me.
So who are these men that have shaped our nation?
Here's 40 or so of whom we'll make a mention!

George Washington, you know he's always number one;
John Adams, number two, moved on to Washington.
Number three, Jefferson, was an inventor and musician;
Number four, Madison, helped write the Constitution.

Monroe and J. Q. Adams were numbers five and six;
Seven, Andrew Jackson, was tough as hickory sticks.
Eight, Van Buren, was a leader during tough times;
Tyler and Will Harrison were presidents ten and nine.

James Polk, number 11, helped acquire more land;
Number 12, Zach Taylor, worked to protect the Union.
Thirteen, Millard Fillmore, helped us all to "compromise";
Fourteen, Franklin Pierce, had nonslave states choose sides.

Fifteen, Buchanan, tried to prevent the Civil War;
Sixteen, Honest Abe, said, "Slavery no more!"
Seventeen, Andrew Johnson, tried to help the South;
Eighteen, Grant's a general not to be left out.

Nineteen, Hayes, thought the telephone truly unique;
Twenty, James Garfield, wrote in both Latin and Greek.
Twenty-one, Chester Arthur, helped the navy even more;
Twenty-two, Grover Cleveland, was also 24!

Twenty-three, Harrison, was called Little Ben;
McKinley, 25, wanted the U.S. great again.
Twenty-six, Roosevelt, was a true "teddy bear";
Taft, 27, on the lawn had cows there.

Twenty-eight, Woodrow Wilson, tried hard to keep from war;
Harding, 29, wanted world peace once more.
Thirty, Calvin Coolidge, was known as Silent Cal;
Thirty-one, Hoover's "depression" is still remembered now.

F.D.R., 32, by the fire liked to chat;
Thirty-three, Harry Truman, World War II he was at.
Thirty-four, Eisenhower, was a general, you bet;
Kennedy, 35, was the youngest yet.

Thirty-six, Johnson, gave a vote that was the right move;
Thirty-seven, Nixon, made foreign relations improve.
Gerald Ford, 38, and 39 was Carter;
Forty, Ronald Reagan, was a great communicator.

George Bush, 41, foreign affairs filled his days;
Forty-two, Clinton, the saxophone he played.
George W. Bush completes the "Famous 43";
Who is in the future? Perhaps it could be you or me!

Note to the teacher: Use with "Presidential Rap" on page 54.

Charts: collecting data

Farmer George's Data Chart

Seed Name	Date Planted	Date of Germination	Amount of Water Required	Date of Maturity	Health of Plant
Wheat					
Corn					
Oats					
Barley					

©The Education Center, Inc. • FEBRUARY • TEC207

Note to the teacher: Use this page with "Farmer George?" on page 56.

Book Talk Map

Use this Book Talk Map to organize your ideas and thoughts. Use it as a reference during your oral presentation.

Title: _____

Author: _____

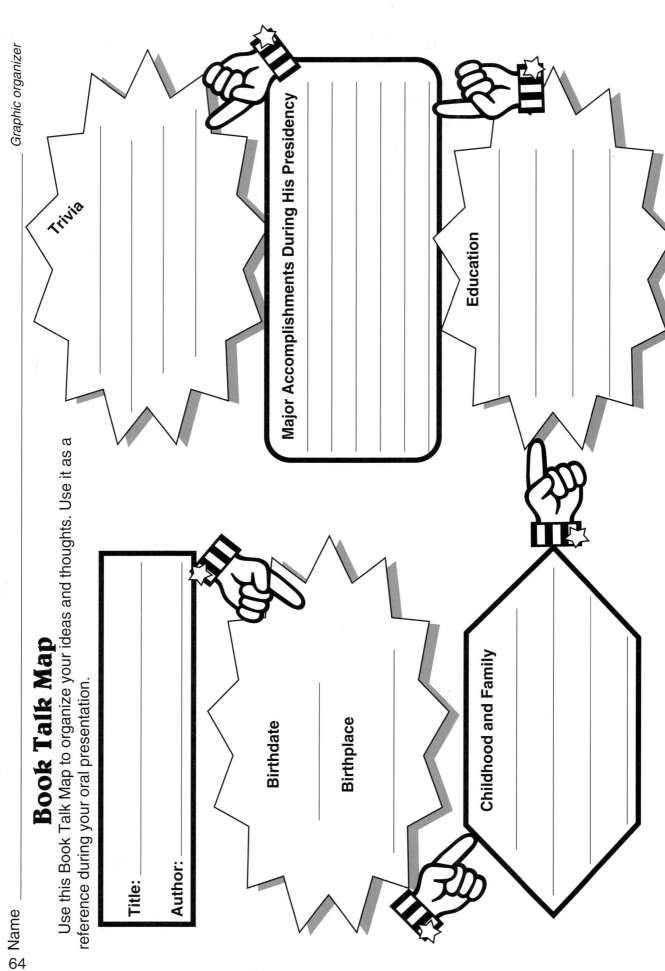

Trivia

Major Accomplishments During His Presidency

Education

Birthdate _____

Birthplace _____

Childhood and Family

Note to the teacher: Use with "Talking Tales" on page 60.

Presidential Fitness and Fun

The following presidents enjoyed a variety of sports. Research to match each sport below with at least one president from the list. When you've found a match, write the president's name in the appropriate box. Each president may be used more than once.

George W. Bush
William Clinton
George Bush
Ronald Reagan
James Carter
Gerald Ford
Richard Nixon
Lyndon Johnson
John Kennedy
Dwight Eisenhower
Harry Truman
Franklin Roosevelt
Herbert Hoover

Calvin Coolidge
Warren Harding
Woodrow Wilson
William Taft
Theodore Roosevelt
William McKinley
Benjamin Harrison
Grover Cleveland
Chester Arthur
James Garfield
Rutherford Hayes
Ulysses Grant
Abraham Lincoln

James Buchanan
Franklin Pierce
Zachary Taylor
John Tyler
William Henry Harrison
Martin Van Buren
Andrew Jackson
John Q. Adams
James Monroe
James Madison
Thomas Jefferson
John Adams
George Washington

Swimming	Jogging	Golf	Bicycling
Touch Football	**Horseback Riding**	**Fishing**	**Hunting**
Walking	**Ice-Skating**	**Tennis**	**Horseshoes**
Bowling	**Softball**	**Speedboating**	**Skiing**

Bonus Box: Do you think that the president should participate in sports while in office? Why or why not?

©The Education Center, Inc. • *FEBRUARY* • TEC207 • Key p. 93

Note to the teacher: Use this page with "Fitness and Fun" on page 61.

Race for the White House

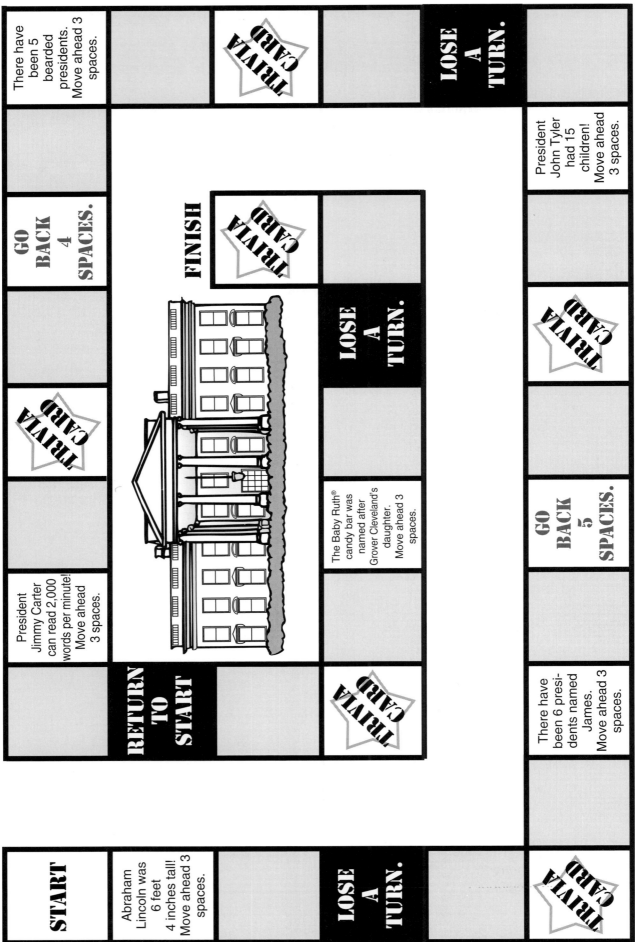

There have been 5 bearded presidents. Move ahead 3 spaces.

TRIVIA CARD

LOSE A TURN.

President John Tyler had 15 children! Move ahead 3 spaces.

GO BACK 4 SPACES.

FINISH

TRIVIA CARD

TRIVIA CARD

TRIVIA CARD

LOSE A TURN.

President Jimmy Carter can read 2,000 words per minute! Move ahead 3 spaces.

The Baby Ruth® candy bar was named after Grover Cleveland's daughter. Move ahead 3 spaces.

GO BACK 5 SPACES.

RETURN TO START

TRIVIA CARD

There have been 6 presidents named James. Move ahead 3 spaces.

START

Abraham Lincoln was 6 feet 4 inches tall! Move ahead 3 spaces.

LOSE A TURN.

TRIVIA CARD

©The Education Center, Inc. • FEBRUARY • TEC207

Note to the teacher: Use with "Trivia Trek" on page 63 and "Race for the White House Trivia Card" on page 67.

Race for the White House Trivia Card

1. Which president is pictured on the $1,000 bill?
   (Grover Cleveland)

2. In which state were more presidents born than in any other state?
   (Virginia)

3. Which president invented the swivel chair?
   (Thomas Jefferson)

4. Which president resigned from office?
   (Richard Nixon)

5. Who was the shortest president?
   (James Madison—5 feet, 4 inches)

6. What was George Washington's yearly salary as president?
   ($25,000)

7. Which president was previously an actor?
   (Ronald Reagan)

8. How many children did George Washington have?
   (None. His wife had children from a previous marriage whom he adopted.)

9. Which president is pictured on the $5,000 bill?
   (James Madison)

10. Which president was first to live in the White House?
    (John Adams)

11. Which four presidents have their faces carved on Mount Rushmore?
    (George Washington, Thomas Jefferson, Theodore Roosevelt, and Abraham Lincoln)

12. Which three presidents have lived to be 90 years old?
    (John Adams, Herbert Hoover, and Ronald Reagan)

13. Which president was the first to be born in the twentieth century?
    (John F. Kennedy)

14. How many presidents have died on the Fourth of July and what are their names?
    (Three: John Adams, Thomas Jefferson, and James Monroe)

15. Which president served the shortest term as president?
    (William H. Harrison—32 days in office)

16. Who was the youngest person elected president?
    (John F. Kennedy was 43 when he was elected president.)

17. How many states are named for presidents?
    (Only one—Washington)

18. Which president served longer than any other president?
    (Franklin D. Roosevelt. He was elected to four terms.)

19. What job did most of the presidents have before being elected to office?
    (Most were lawyers.)

20. Which president kept a cow on the White House grounds for fresh milk?
    (William H. Taft)

21. Who was the first president to wear long pants instead of knickers or knee breeches?
    (James Madison)

22. At what age was George Washington completely toothless?
    (57 years old)

23. Which six presidents are found on U.S. coins?
    (Abraham Lincoln, George Washington, Thomas Jefferson, Franklin D. Roosevelt, John F. Kennedy, and Dwight D. Eisenhower)

24. Which president was the first person in the United States to grow a tomato?
    (Thomas Jefferson)

25. Who was the first president not born in the original 13 colonies?
    (Abraham Lincoln)

26. Who is the only president to serve two nonconsecutive terms?
    (Grover Cleveland)

27. Name at least one state capital named after a president.
    (Jackson, Mississippi; Jefferson City, Missouri; Lincoln, Nebraska; and Madison, Wisconsin)

28. Who is the earliest president of whom a photograph exists?
    (John Quincy Adams)

29. Which president smoked 20 cigars a day?
    (Ulysses S. Grant)

30. Who was the first president for whom women could vote?
    (Warren G. Harding)

Presidential Nicknames

Did you know that almost every president has had a nickname? Some presidents received their nicknames as children, whereas others received their nicknames while serving in office. Use reference books to help you match each nickname below with the correct president. Can you find all 20?

Presidents	Nicknames
1. _____ Bill Clinton	A. Old Rough and Ready
2. _____ Richard Nixon	B. Handsome Frank
3. _____ William Howard Taft	C. Ten-Cent Jimmy
4. _____ Dwight D. Eisenhower	D. Honest Abe
5. _____ Andrew Jackson	E. Uncle Sam
6. _____ Zachary Taylor	F. His Fraudulency
7. _____ Grover Cleveland	G. Little Ben
8. _____ Franklin Pierce	H. Uncle Jumbo
9. _____ Ulysses S. Grant	I. Wobbly Willie
10. _____ Benjamin Harrison	J. Red Fox
11. _____ Abraham Lincoln	K. Old Hickory
12. _____ Ronald Reagan	L. Young Hickory
13. _____ Woodrow Wilson	M. Big Bill
14. _____ Herbert Hoover	N. Chief
15. _____ James Knox Polk	O. Ike
16. _____ George Bush	P. Tricky Dick
17. _____ Thomas Jefferson	Q. Dutch
18. _____ James Buchanan	R. Poppy
19. _____ Rutherford B. Hayes	S. Bubba
20. _____ William McKinley	T. Professor

Nicknames often reflect an individual's personality, appearance, career, title, or good deeds. Look at the people listed below. Create a nickname for each person using the positive qualities of their personalities, appearances, careers, titles, or good deeds. Compare your nicknames with those created by your classmates. Are they similar or different?

Your teacher: _____

The principal of your school: _____

Your parent or guardian: _____

Bonus Box: Do you have a nickname? If so, explain how and why you received it. If you do not have a nickname, create one for yourself; then explain why you chose this particular nickname.

©The Education Center, Inc. • *FEBRUARY* • TEC207 • Key p. 93

68   **Note to the teacher:** Divide students into pairs. Make one copy of this page for each pair. Provide a variety of reference materials.

Presidential Firsts

Did you know that Thomas Jefferson's grandson was the first baby born in the White House? Did you know that Harry Truman was the first president to travel underwater in a modern submarine? Use the clues and your research skills to find more unusual presidential firsts. (There are no spaces between first and last names in the puzzle, and three of the names include initials.)

Across

1 First president to have been divorced.
2 First president to have been a Rhodes scholar.
4 First president to use electricity in the White House.
12 First president to appear on television.
16 First president to resign his office.
17 First president to wear a beard in office.
18 First president to fly in an airplane.

Down

1 First president to use a phone in the White House.
3 First president to be sworn in by a female.
5 First president to be the father of another president.
6 First president to speak on the radio.
7 First and only president to get a speeding ticket while riding a horse.
8 First president to have been a Boy Scout.
9 First president to have an asteroid named after him.
10 First president to refuse publicly to eat broccoli.
11 First and only president who was never married.
13 First president to appear on a postage stamp.
14 First president to ride a train.
15 First president to be born in a hospital.

Bonus Box: Of the presidential firsts listed above, which do you think is the most important? Why?

The Quest for Better Letters

Activities for Teaching Letter-Writing Skills

Let neither snow, nor rain, nor heat, nor gloom of night keep you from your appointed duty of pursuing better letter-writing skills! Honor the anniversary of the creation of the U.S. Post Office on February 20, 1792, by delivering these first-class activities to your students.

by Beverly Cartledge and Paula Holdren

Literature for the Pursuit

Embark on your quest by opening this mailbag full of great resources and read-alouds. Right at your fingertips are suggestions for great fiction; resources that give addresses of movie stars, athletes, clubs, organizations, publications, musicians, and kid-related businesses and products; and books that provide students with examples, models, and advice for writing all kinds of letters. So charge ahead!

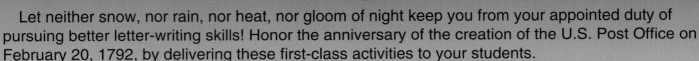

Resources
The Kid's Address Book edited by Michael Levine
Putting It in Writing by Steve Otfinoski
Messages in the Mailbox: How to Write a Letter by Loreen Leedy
Free Stuff for Kids, editions updated yearly

Read-Alouds
Anastasia at This Address by Lois Lowry
Dear Mr. Henshaw by Beverly Cleary
Dear Napoleon, I Know You're Dead, But… by Elvira Woodruff

Letters Are Our Bag!

Letters Are Our Bag!

Create an eye-catching bulletin board for your letter-writing unit. Before starting the unit, ask students to bring in samples of junk mail and other miscellaneous items from daily home-mail deliveries. Follow the directions below to make a mail pouch from a paper grocery bag. Stuff the bag with the mail samples brought in by the students; then staple the mailbag to one side of a bulletin board under the title. Arrange additional pieces of mail around the outside of the pouch. Add student letter samples to the board as the unit progresses.

To make the mail pouch:

1. Cut the top six inches off a brown paper grocery bag (Figure 1).
2. Trim the cut-off piece to make a 2" x 18" strip (Figure 2).
3. Cut the remaining grocery bag in half at the sides to create front and back halves (Figure 3).
4. Turn the front and back halves inside out so that all print is on the inside.
5. Fit the two halves together, overlapping the sides and bottoms to create a pouch that is half the thickness of the original bag.
6. Tape the two halves together at the sides and at the bottom.
7. Attach each end of the 18-inch strip to the inner sides of the pouch to create a handle.
8. Use a black marker to add stitching lines to the outside of the bag and to the handle (Figure 4). Label the front of the bag "U.S. Mail."

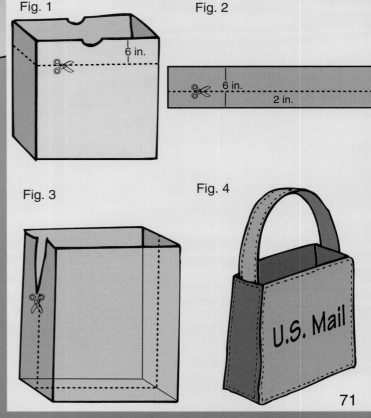

Fig. 1   6 in.

Fig. 2   6 in.   2 in.

Fig. 3

Fig. 4   U.S. Mail

Expressly for Me
Making a personal connection
Encourage students to be more prolific letter writers by allowing them to create personalized stationery. Give each student several sheets of copy paper; then ask her to design a decorative border or logo that reflects her personality. Or allow the student to use computer clip art to create a design. Once her design is complete, duplicate several sheets of the paper for her to keep. Suggest that she use it to write to a friend or relative, or to request some freebies from one of the resources listed on page 70.

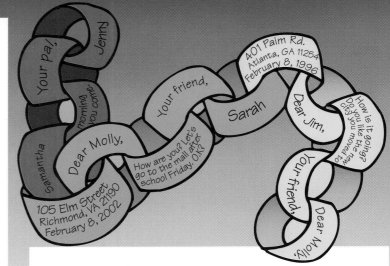

Chain Letter
Writing a friendly letter
Strengthen the links in students' letter-writing skills by having them create paper "chain" letters! Place your students' names in a hat, have each student draw a classmate's name, and then have him write a friendly letter to that classmate. Remind the student to include the heading, greeting, body, closing, and signature in his letter. Caution the student to keep the body of his letter short. Gather a supply of colorful 12" x 18" paper. Give each student a ruler, scissors, and a sheet of paper. Have the student cut his paper into five 12" x 2 1/2" strips. Instruct the student to use a pen or fine-tipped marker to copy his letter's heading onto the first strip, the greeting onto the second, the body onto the third, and so on. Direct the student to staple his first four strips together in sequence as shown. Have the student paper-clip the fifth strip together until he's asked to connect it to another student's chain. Assist students with stapling the separate chains together to make one long chain. Do not connect two chains of the same color. String the completed chain around your classroom, on a bulletin board, or down a hallway to create a display that won't be "returned to sender!"

Don't Forget the Stamp! 🖳
Generating correspondence, using map skills

Have you ever wished that you could crawl inside an envelope and mail yourself to another place in the United States? Let students do just that with this adventurous activity. Read aloud *Flat Stanley* by Jeff Brown. Stanley is a boy who, after being flattened by a falling bulletin board, mails himself to California to visit a friend. Invite each student to choose a place in the United States that he would like to visit. Duplicate the person pattern on page 76 and the reply form on page 77 for each student. Instruct the student to illustrate the pattern to look like himself; then have him place the illustrated pattern, along with the reply form, in an envelope so that it can be mailed to a friend or relative in another U.S. town. In addition, have the student enclose a stamped, self-addressed envelope and a note requesting that his friend photograph the pattern visiting some fun places. Make sure that the student asks his friend to send him the photographs when he mails back the pattern and the reply form. Mount a U.S. map on a bulletin board. As the traveling patterns return, mark the spots they visited on the map using small colored stickers. Display the flat travelers along with the replies and photographs around the map. As students read about the adventures, they'll *really* wish they'd been there!

Wish You Were Here! 🖳
Descriptive writing

What a thrill it is to get a postcard from an exotic place! Have students practice sending brief messages by writing postcards. Give each student a postcard form from page 77. Have the student pretend she is vacationing anyplace in the world. Instruct the student to write her friend a postcard that briefly describes something she's done, seen, or eaten while on this once-in-a-lifetime trip. Be sure the student also includes an illustration of the vacation spot on the back of the postcard!

Lady Sarah
Coatsworth Castle
London, England

Greetings and Salutations
Writing for a purpose

Make it easy for students to use letter-writing skills in everyday situations. Set up a classroom center from which birthday, sympathy, and get-well cards can be written. Ask students to bring in the front portions of old greeting cards. Store the card fronts in a special box at a center along with colored paper, glue, scissors, and fine-tipped markers. Duplicate a copy of the tips on page 78; then post it at the center. When a student feels that a classmate or another school friend needs a greeting card, allow him to visit the center during free time. After selecting and gluing an appropriate card front to folded construction paper, have him write a personal message inside and deliver it. The student delivering the greeting card will experience as much satisfaction as the one receiving it!

Dear Sammy,
My class is learning how to write letters. I am sending you a pattern that ...painted to look like me! Please ...ve him and call him by my ...at a fun place

R. S. V. P.
Your name: _____

Pen-Pal Connections
Making a personal connection, writing a friendly letter

Who says pen pals have to live far away? Request a listing of schools and addresses from your school system's central office. Write to several of the schools requesting a pen-pal class. After finding a willing class, pair the pals and let the letter writing begin. If both your school and your pen pals' school have email addresses, allow students to correspond via the Internet. Have each student share information about classroom studies, school or community activities, and personal interests in his letters. After the classes have exchanged letters several times, arrange for a joint curriculum-related field trip so that the two classes can meet.

Stuffable Stamps 🖥
Following directions

What do Elvis, Marilyn Monroe, angels, and airplanes have in common? They've all been pictured on postage stamps! Ignite more interest in letter writing by having students design stamps. Ask each student to bring in two inexpensive, large, white cotton handkerchiefs (available at discount department stores). Give each student a 14-inch cardboard square, a 12-inch square of waxed paper, masking tape, a paintbrush, colorful fabric paint, and one handkerchief. Then have the student follow these steps:

1. Layer the waxed paper between the cardboard and the handkerchief to keep the paint from sticking to the cardboard.
2. Wrap the handkerchief's edges around the cardboard and secure with masking tape as shown.
3. Sketch a design in pencil—first on paper and then on the handkerchief—that honors a person, place, thing, or event.
4. Paint over the design on the handkerchief with fabric paints; then allow the paint to dry for 24 hours.
5. Remove the handkerchief from the cardboard.

Enlist a parent to sew each student's designed handkerchief to a second blank handkerchief, leaving an opening for stuffing the pillow with fiberfill. After each student has stuffed and sewn closed the opening on his pillow, let him prop himself on it to write a thank-you note to the seamstress!

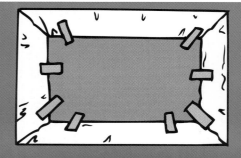

Immediate Results
Writing a business letter

Emphasize the purpose of business letters with a fun, cooperative letter-writing activity. Make a list of local businesses that provide services or products that appeal to students. Explain to students that the general goal of a business letter is to place an order, register a complaint, or request information. Review with students the correct form and rules for writing a business letter. Pair students. Then have each pair choose the name of one business from the list. Instruct the partners to brainstorm a list of complaints that could be lodged against that business. Have one partner take the role of customer while the other partner role-plays the business owner. Direct the "customer" to write to the "business owner." Then have the "owner" respond back in writing. Give each pair two colored sheets of paper on which to mount these two letters. Then have the pair tape the letters together at the top so that the second letter can be read by lifting up the first. Display the letters by draping them over a length of string.

Priority Mail
Writing a business letter

Channel students' concerns about current events into positive actions by having them write business letters. First have students brainstorm issues that concern them. List the students' ideas on the board under four categories—*school, community, state,* and *national.* Divide students into groups. Have each group choose one topic of concern from each category. Instruct each group to carefully word four business letters, addressing each one to the person who could answer the concern. For instance, the group could send a letter about its school concern to the principal or president of the PTA, a letter about its community concern to the mayor or to the editor of the local newspaper, a letter about its state concern to the governor, and a letter about its national concern to a congressman or to the president. Help students conclude that they have the right to voice their opinions about the issues that affect their daily lives.

Pattern

Use with "Don't Forget the Stamp!" on page 73.

R. S. V. P.

Your name: _____

The name of your flat-friend visitor: _____

The city and state in which you live: _____

_____

A description of the area in which you live:

_____

_____

Things you did to entertain your visitor: _____

_____

_____

How you felt about participating in this activity: _____

_____

_____

©The Education Center, Inc. • *FEBRUARY* • TEC207

Note to the teacher: Use this form with "Don't Forget the Stamp!" on page 73.

Pattern
Use with "Wish You Were Here!" on page 73.

©The Education Center, Inc. • *FEBRUARY* • TEC207

Tips for Writing...

Thank-You Notes

Write a thank-you note in the form of a friendly letter when you…
- receive a gift. Let the giver know his gift was received and is appreciated.
- receive a gift of money. Let the giver know that the money was received and how it will be used.
- stay overnight at the home of another person. Thank him for his hospitality.
- are treated by another person to a meal in a restaurant or in a home. Thank him for his generosity or compliment him on his cooking talents.

> February 23
>
> Dear Aunt Guinevere,
>   Thank you for sending me those delicious homemade cookies. My friends said they were the best ones they'd ever eaten!
>
>   Your nephew,
>   Bertrand

Get-Well Cards

Write a get-well message in the form of a friendly letter to a person who:
- is sick at home.
- has been in the hospital recuperating from an illness or an operation.
- has been injured.

Let the person know that you're thinking about him. Keep your message positive and encouraging.

> February 16
>
> Dear Bertrand,
>   I'm sorry you broke your arm falling off your horse at Jousting School. I hope you'll soon be up and at 'em again!
>
>   Your cousin,
>   Bernadette

Sympathy Cards

Write a note of sympathy in the form of a friendly letter to someone when:
- her close friend or relative dies.
- her pet dies.

Keep your message brief. Let the person know that you are thinking of her and her family during their time of grief. Share something nice that you remember about the person or pet that has passed away.

> February 19
>
> Dear Bernadette,
>   I was so sorry to hear that your grandfather died. He was so much fun to be around. Please give my sympathy to the rest of your family.
>
>   Sincerely,
>   Bertrand

Notes of Apology

Write a letter of apology in the form of a friendly letter when:
- you do something you should not have done.
- you say something you should not have said.

In the letter, admit your mistake and say you are sorry. Offer to do something to make things right again.

> February 10
>
> Dear Mom,
>   I'm sorry my pet dragon burned a hole in the rug. I'll do extra chores around the castle to make up for it.
>
>   Love,
>   Bertrand

Congratulations

Send good wishes in the form of a friendly letter when someone you know:
- has a birthday.
- moves into a new home.
- gets a new baby brother or sister.
- graduates from high school or college.
- receives an award or special recognition.

Let your friend know how happy you are for him.

> February 15
>
> Dear Bernadette,
>   Congratulations on winning the castle's Best Seamstress Award. I didn't know you were so talented! By the way, I could use some padding for my armor!
>
>   Your cousin,
>   Bertrand

Note to the teacher: Use this page with "Greetings and Salutations" on page 73. Post these writing tips at a center as described or duplicate a copy for each student to keep inside a writing folder.

The Post Office cannot deliver letters if they have incorrect or incomplete addresses. Such letters go to the Dead-Mail Office. Look at the six envelopes below. See if you can save these letters from being tossed into a dead-letter bin. Each envelope has one or more errors written on the main address. Make up the appropriate information that will correct the main address. Remember that every address needs a full name, street or P.O. box, city, state, and zip code. Sometimes an address will need both a name and place before the street. Other addresses may need apartment numbers.

Elma Birchwood
63 Oak Ln.
Willow Bend, CA 97809

Ace Tree Service

Austin, TX

1.

Mike Myron
26 State Street
Trenton, NJ 49870

Chris

Reading, PA

2.

Max Tomas
21-B Satellite Apts.
4555 Antenna Road
Lincoln, NE 50678

Zack's TV Repair
Cottonwood Dr.
Lincoln, NE

3.

Marlin Fish
1 Outtawatta Pl.
Miami, FL 39876

The Bay City Times
P.O.
Tampa

4.

Miss Ima Jones
88 Keepinup Way
Phoenix, AZ 89045

Mrs. T. Smythe
Apt. #
2223 Vista
Fresno, CA

5.

S. Salamander
519 Swamp St.
Asheboro, NC 29876

Mary Monkey
The Zoo
Route 60
Chesterfield,   23838

6.

Bonus Box: Draw an envelope shape on the back of this sheet. Make up a name, address, and zip code for a radio station in New York City. Use them to address the envelope. Remember to include your return address.

Weather Magic

Looking for a few tricks to pull out of your hat for a weather unit? Use the following activities and your students will be spouting weather lore before you can say "abracadabra!"

by Liz Lindsay

It's easy to talk about the weather. That's because the word *weather* describes the condition of our atmosphere—the air that surrounds us all. As the sun and the earth interact, they make changes in the atmosphere's *temperature, pressure, wind,* and *moisture.* Over time, and with more scientific equipment, *meteorologists*—scientists who study weather—have learned to recognize the signs that help predict the weather. As a result, we have become more accurate in our forecasting and in our understanding.

Fascinating Facts
Building background knowledge

Mesmerize your students with these fascinating facts about weather! Obtain a magician's top hat from a party store or make a three-dimensional model from black paper or cardboard and paint. Then make a two-dimensional top hat from black paper and post it on the wall. Make one copy of the fact sheet and 15 copies of the rabbit pattern from page 87. Cut out each fact and glue it to a cutout pattern. Then place the facts in the three-dimensional hat. Each day during the week before your weather unit begins, have three student volunteers pull one rabbit each from the hat and read the weather fact. Post each fact on the wall beside the two-dimensional top hat.

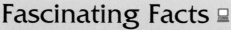

The Little Book of Weather Words
Understanding vocabulary

Unlock the secrets of weather words by creating mini vocabulary booklets. Provide each student with 28 plain white index cards (either 4" x 6" or 5" x 7"). Have each student use a hole puncher to poke two holes along one of the longer sides of each card. Instruct each student to label a front cover card with the title, her name, and an illustration. Then have her set aside another card for the back cover. Finally, have her label the top of each of the remaining cards with a letter of the alphabet. Pass around a skein of yarn and instruct each student to cut two six-inch lengths. Have each student bind her cards together using the yarn. As you introduce a new vocabulary word, have each student add that term, its definition, and an illustration to the appropriate card in her booklet.

Listed below are some suggested weather words:

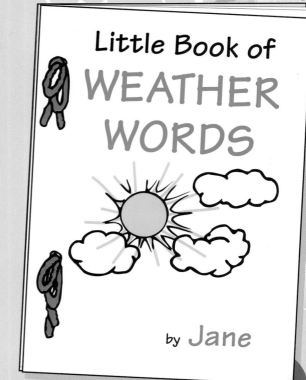

A: air mass, air pressure, anemometer, atmosphere; **B:** barometer, Beaufort scale; **C:** Celsius, climate, cloud, condensation; **D:** data, dew; **E:** evaporation; **F:** Fahrenheit, fog, forecast, front; **G:** global warming; **H:** humidity, hurricane, hygrometer; **I:** isobar; **J:** jet stream; **K:** knot; **L:** lightning; **M:** meteorologist, molecule; **N:** National Weather Service; **O:** observation station; **P:** precipitation, prediction; **R:** radar, rainbow, rain gauge; **S:** satellite, storm; **T:** temperature, thermometer, thunderstorm, tornado; **U:** updraft; **V:** vapor, visibility; **W:** warning, watch, weather, weather map, wind, wind vane; **Z:** zone

How's the Weather?
Identifying cause and effect relationships

No Houdini can escape the effects of weather in our lives. Help students understand the causes and effects related to weather. Bring in a supply of daily newspapers and newsmagazines. Begin a discussion by brainstorming the ways weather affects (1) how we work and play, (2) what we eat, and (3) the moods we feel. Divide students into small groups and have each group locate and cut out three to four news articles that relate to weather in any part of the world. Share an example, such as an announcement about school closings due to snow, or a report on increased food prices due to weather-damaged crops. Have each group read its articles, underlining the weather causes and circling the effects of the weather. Then have each group post its articles around a map of the United States or the world. Use yarn to attach each article to the location of the weather occurrence.

The Heat Is On!

Observing direct and indirect light

Hot or cold, summer or winter—each, in part, is determined by the angle of the sun's rays on a given location on the earth's surface. Demonstrate this concept using a flashlight and a blackboard. First, turn off the lights and shine the flashlight directly onto the blackboard's surface. Have a student trace around the lighted area using chalk. Next, hold the flashlight so that it shines on the board at a 45° angle. Have another student trace this new lighted area. Turn on the lights and have students compare the area lighted by the direct ray of the flashlight to that of the indirect ray. Point out that the more direct the sun's rays, the more intense the light and the heat.

Blowing in the Wind

Creating a model of circulating air

From gentle breezes to hurricanes, the winds in our atmosphere result simply from differences in temperature and air pressure. As the sun warms the atmosphere, the heated air moves upward and the colder air moves into its place. This exchange causes molecules in the air to circulate, creating wind. Demonstrate this process with the following model:

Materials: shoebox without a lid; votive candle; damp, wadded-up paper towel; small glass plate; cellophane; matches; scissors; tape

Directions:

1. Turn the shoebox on its side and make three cuts (see diagram):
   a. Cut out a 3/4" hole at one end of the box.
   b. Cut a hinged door at the other end of the box.
   c. Cut out a 3/4" hole over to one side of the "top" of the box.
2. Place the candle under the top hole as shown.
3. Stretch cellophane over the large opening, securing it with tape so that no air escapes. (You will observe the experiment through the cellophane.)
4. Set the damp paper towel on the plate. Put the plate next to the box outside the side hole.
5. Open the hinged door and light the candle.
6. Light the dampened towel. (Inform students that they will have to watch carefully, as the results happen quickly.)
7. Observe the direction of the smoke from the paper towel.

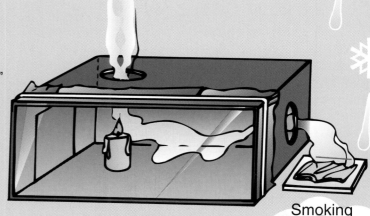

Box With Cellophane Front

Smoking Towel

The lighted candle will warm the air inside the box. The warm air will rise out the top hole, creating a vacuum. Colder air will rush inside the box from the side hole, carrying with it the smoke from the burning paper.

Now You See Them, Now You Don't

Observing how rainbows form

Do you make a wish when you see a rainbow? If so, you know that you have to act fast. Rainbows tend to appear and disappear very quickly. They form during or right after a shower when the sun has just broken through the clouds. They always appear on the side of the sky that is opposite to the sun. Help students understand the origin of rainbows with this simple demonstration. Turn off the lights and place a clear glass filled with water on a lighted overhead projector. Have students observe the shafts of colored light. Explain that light usually appears white to us, but when the rays of white light hit the curved water droplets in the sky, the droplets act like prisms, bending the light into its spectrum of colors: *red, orange, yellow, green, blue, indigo,* and *violet.*

A Fog Is Born

Observing how fog forms

Not every cloud has a silver lining. But every cloud does contain tiny droplets of water. The cloud is formed when tiny droplets of water join around the particles in the air. Demonstrate the formation of clouds with the following fog experiment (fog is similiar to clouds, except that it touches the earth's surface, and clouds do not).

Materials: clean, dry, glass bottle; cube of ice large enough to completely cover the mouth of the bottle; cup very hot water; lamp with a 100-watt bulb

Directions:
1. Preheat the bottle with hot tap water to prevent it from breaking.
2. Add a small amount of the hot water to the bottle; then quickly place the large cube of ice over the mouth of the bottle.
3. Shine the lamp on the bottle and observe the air inside.

When held in front of the light, fog will be seen swirling around in the bottle. This happens because the warm, moist air rising in the bottle meets the cool air of the ice cube. Tiny droplets of water form, creating fog.

A Roll of the Dice?
Understanding probability and weather forecasting

At times the weatherman does not seem to have any luck predicting the weather. However, today's technologies enable *meteorologists*—scientists who study and report the weather—to forecast the weather with better accuracy. Use the following activity to help students understand *probability* and to show them that modern weather prediction is more than just "the roll of the dice."

1. Pair students. Make two copies of the die pattern on page 88 for each pair.
2. Instruct each pair to think about the weather patterns that are common at this time of the year. Then have the pair pick five or six of the weather patterns shown on page 88 and cut out and paste one onto each side of the first die. (Remind the partners that if they choose only five of the pictures, they will have to draw an extra pattern in order to fill all six sides of the die.)
3. Instruct each pair to think of six different temperatures—each at least five degrees apart. Have the pair write one temperature on each side of the second die.
4. Have the pairs follow the directions to construct each die.
5. Have the pairs examine their dice as you ask the following questions:
   a. How many possible weather patterns are there? *(Five or six, depending on how many patterns each pair used.)*
   b. Are the outcomes equally likely to occur? *(Pairs that used six different patterns can answer yes. Pairs that used only five patterns will say that the repeated pattern is more likely to occur.)*
   c. How many temperature outcomes are possible? *(Six)*
   d. How many combinations are possible? *(Thirty if the pair used five weather patterns; 36 if the pair used six weather patterns. The answer is found by multiplying the number of weather patterns times the number of temperatures.)*
   e. What are some of those outcomes? *(Answers consist of pairing a weather pattern with a temperature. Answers will vary.)*

Now your students are ready to test the accuracy of modern weather prediction. Duplicate the chart on page 88 for each pair. Have each pair look at the row labeled "Roll of the Dice." Instruct the partners to roll both dice five times and record each combined outcome under a different day of the week in that row. Direct each pair to note the rows labeled "Weatherman's Prediction" and "Actual Weather." Each morning for a week, have the pair record the weatherman's prediction in the appropriate box. Finally, at the end of each day, have the pair record that day's actual weather. At week's end, have each pair compare its roll-of-the-dice predictions with the weatherman's predictions and the actual weather. Based on this short experiment, ask students if they would agree that weather forecasting is based more on science than on probability.

It's All in the Cards 🖥

Reviewing weather facts

Play this hot game to see how well your students have weathered this unit. Duplicate page 89 for each team and cut the four sections apart.

Each team of four will need the following: deck of playing cards, the four-card-suit question/answer sheets (page 89), pencil and paper to add up points

How to play:

1. Have each player choose a card suit to play during the game—*diamonds, hearts, clubs,* or *spades.*
2. Hand each player an answer key for a suit other than his own. (For instance, give the player who chose diamonds the hearts answer key.)
3. Shuffle the deck and place it facedown in the center of the table.
4. In turn have each player draw the top card from the pile and place it faceup next to the pile. This card determines which player answers a question. (For instance, if a spade is drawn, then the player who chose spades as his suit answers a question. The player holding the spades question/answer sheet asks the question.)
5. If the question is answered correctly, the player who answered keeps the card and earns the number of points shown on the card. The face cards are worth the following: Jack = 11, Queen = 12, King = 13, and Ace = 15.
6. If the player answers incorrectly, the card is placed into a discard pile.
7. Play continues until all the cards have been drawn and the questions have been answered. (Each player will have had 13 questions.)
8. The player earning the most points wins the game.

Wet As a Rag
or Dry As a Bone?

Collecting and graphing data, writing for a purpose

The amount of precipitation that a city receives can seriously impact the lives of its inhabitants. Brainstorm with the class problems that would occur from either too much or too little rainfall. Select a nearby city to research. Check an almanac, or contact the local weather bureau or television station for a list of the annual precipitation amounts for that city over the last ten years. Help students graph this data. Then have each student follow up his findings by writing a business letter to one of the various weather-related local or state agencies. In the letter, have the student request information on how that agency deals with emergency storm, drought, or flood conditions.

Mary Gates, New Milford, CT

Let the Show Begin!

Researching a topic, writing to inform

No Broadway show can compare to the magnificent display of power and fury unleashed by Mother Nature during a storm. Alert students to the facts about storms that occur in their region by forming Storm Alert Teams. Assign each of three teams one of the following storms: *tornadoes, hurricanes,* or *electrical storms.* Direct each team to research the *what, where, when, why,* and *how* facts about its storm. Then have each team find out how people can protect themselves during this particular type of storm.

Share this useful information with the entire school by displaying the research on a hallway bulletin board or wall space. Divide a large board or wall space into three sections, one for each of the three teams. Have each team summarize its findings and write them on attractive cards or banners. Direct each team to include illustrations to go with its facts. If desired, spread the message of storm severity by having each team create a short skit showcasing the dangers and precautions that are important to that storm. Have your Storm Alert Teams travel from class to class presenting this vital information.

LIGHTNING DON'TS

1. Don't go under a tree that stands alone.

2. Don't use electrical appliances.

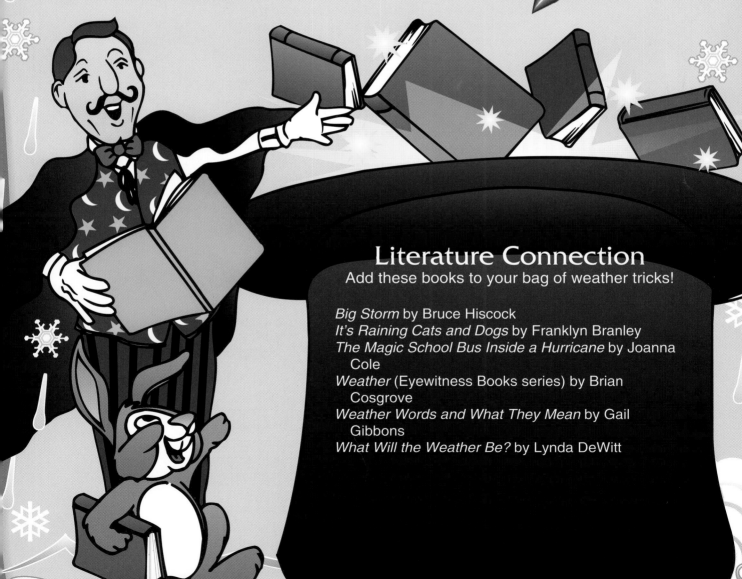

Literature Connection

Add these books to your bag of weather tricks!

Big Storm by Bruce Hiscock
It's Raining Cats and Dogs by Franklyn Branley
The Magic School Bus Inside a Hurricane by Joanna Cole
Weather (Eyewitness Books series) by Brian Cosgrove
Weather Words and What They Mean by Gail Gibbons
What Will the Weather Be? by Lynda DeWitt